Pellet Grill Cookbook

125 Award-Winning Pellet Grilling BBQ

Recipes for the Best Barbeque

Gregory Moore

Copyright © 2017 by Northern Press

All rights Reserved. This book or any portion thereof may not be reproduced or used in any manner whatsoever without the express written permission of the publisher except for the use of brief quotation in a book review. The scanning, uploading, and distribution of this book via the Internet or via any other means without the permission of the publisher is illegal and punishable by law.

Please purchase only authorized editions of this book and don't participate in or encourage electronic piracy of copyrighted materials.

If you would like to share this book with another person, please purchase an additional copy for each person you share it with, or ask them to buy their own recipes. This was hard work for the author and he appreciates it.

This book is solely for information and education purposes and is not medical advice. Please consult a medical or health professional before you begin any exercise, nutrition, or supplementation program or if you have questions about your health.

Specific results mentioned in this book should be considered extraordinary and there are no "typical" results. As individuals differ, then results will differ.

ISBN-13: 978-1977589545

ISBN-10: 1977589545

Published by Northern Press Inc.

Table of contents

Festive Whole Chicken (6 servings, serving: 1 portion) 8

Entrée Chicken (4 servings, serving: 1 portion) 9

Christmas Dinner Chicken (4 servings, serving: 1 portion) 10

Super-Tasty Chicken Drumsticks (6 servings, serving: 1 portion) 11

Divine Chicken Drumsticks (8 servings, serving: 1 portion) 12

Decadent Chicken Drumsticks (6 servings, serving: 1 portion) 13

Drunken Drumsticks (8 servings, serving: 1 portion) 14

Super-Easy Chicken Quarters (8 servings, serving: 1 portion) 15

Awesome Chicken Quarters (6 servings, serving: 1 portion) 16

Juicy Chicken Thighs (6 servings, serving: 1 portion) 17

Flavorsome Chicken Thighs (4 servings, serving: 1 portion) 18

Luscious Chicken Breasts (6 servings, serving: 1 portion) 19

Weeknight Chicken Breasts (6 servings, serving: 1 portion) 20

Exotic Chicken Breasts (4 servings, serving: 1 portion) 21

Flavored Chicken Wings (4 servings, serving: 1 portion) 22

Asian Inspired Chicken Wings (4 servings, serving: 1 portion) 23

Summertime Dinner Hens (4 servings, serving: 1 portion) 24

Favorite Whole Turkey (16 servings, serving: 1 portion) 25

Thanksgiving Turkey (12 servings, serving: 1 portion) 26

Family Dinner Turkey (16 servings, serving: 1 portion) 27

Simplest Turkey Breast (12 servings, serving: 1 portion) 28

Glazed Turkey Breast (6 servings, serving: 1 portion) 30

Sunday Dinner Turkey Legs (6 servings, serving: 1 portion) 31

Standard Turkey Legs (4 servings, serving: 1 portion) 32

Simply Perfect Duck (6 servings, serving: 1 portion) 33

Crispy Duck (6 servings, serving: 1 portion) 34

2 ingredients Dinner (4 servings, serving: 1 portion) 35

Irresistible Duck Legs (8 servings, serving: 1 portion) 36

Fancy Dinner Goose (12 servings, serving: 1 portion) 37

Sweet & Tangy Goose Breast (8 servings, serving: 1 portion) 39

Succulent Beef Tenderloin (12 servings, serving: 1 portion) 40

Versatile Beef Tenderloin (6 servings, serving: 1 portion) 41

Delish Rib Roast (10 servings, serving: 1 portion) 42

Aromatic Rib Roast (12 servings, serving: 1 portion) 43

Simply Tasty Roast (8 servings, serving: 1 portion) 44

Special Dinner Roast (8 servings, serving: 1 portion) 45

Stunning Rump Roast (8 servings, serving: 1 portion) 46

Deliciously Spicy Roast (6 servings, serving: 1 portion) 47

Simple-Ever Chuck Roast (12 servings, serving: 1 portion) 48

Midweek Dinner Brisket (8 servings, serving: 1 portion) 49

BBQ Party Brisket (12 servings, serving: 1 portion) 50

Easy-to-Prepare Brisket (14 servings, serving: 1 portion) 52

Astonishing Flank Steak (6 servings, serving: 1 portion) 53

Foolproof Strip Steak (2 servings, serving: 1 portion) 54

Elegant Steak (2 servings, serving: 1 portion) 55

American Style Short Ribs (6 servings, serving: 1 portion) 56

Braised Short Ribs (6 servings, serving: 1 portion) 58

Loveable Ribs (4 servings, serving: 1 portion) 59

Greatly Flavored Ribs (4 servings, serving: 1 portion) 60

Healthy Beef Jerky (2-3 servings, serving: 1 portion) 61

Easy Pork Chops (4 servings, serving: 1 portion) 62

Glorious Pork Chops (4 servings, serving: 1 portion) 63

Premium Pork Chops (4 servings, serving: 1 portion) 64

Richly Spicy Pork Ribs (20 servings, serving: 1 portion) 65

Tender Pork Ribs (16 servings, serving: 1 portion) 67
Mouth Watering Pork Ribs (6 servings, serving: 1 portion) 68
Amazing Pork Butt Roast (16 servings, serving: 1 portion) 69
Nicely Flavored Pork Butt Roast (14 servings, serving: 1 portion) 70
Authentic Butt Roast (6 servings, serving: 1 portion) 71
Tender Pork Shoulder (20 servings, serving: 1 portion) 72
Crowd Pleasing Pork Belly (13 servings, serving: 1 portion) 73
Delightfully Perfect Pork Belly (10 servings, serving: 1 portion) 74
Chinese Favorite Pork Belly (10 servings, serving: 1 portion) 75
Welcoming Pork Tenderloin (6 servings, serving: 1 portion) 76
Party Dinner Pork Loin (10 servings, serving: 1 portion) 77
Holiday Special Ham (14 servings, serving: 1 portion) 78
Sweetly Delicious Ham (18 servings, serving: 1 portion) 80
Christmas Table Ham (18 servings, serving: 1 portion) 82
Classic Ham (12 servings, serving: 1 portion) 83
Holiday Feast Ham (24-26 servings, serving: 1 portion) 84
Breakfast Sausage (6 servings, serving: 1 portion) 85
Zesty Sausage (6 servings, serving: 1 portion) 85
Delightful Sausage (5 servings, serving: 1 portion) 86
Enticing Lamb Chops (6 servings, serving: 1 portion) 87
Favorite Lamb Shoulder Chops (4 servings, serving: 1 portion) 88
Irresistible Lamb Ribs Rack (2 servings, serving: 1 portion) 89
Delicious Lamb Ribs Rack (8 servings, serving: 1 portion) 90
Spice Crusted Ribs Rack (4 servings, serving: 1 portion) 91
Effortless Lamb Ribs Rack (3 servings, serving: 1 portion) 92
Distinctive Lamb Shank (6 servings, serving: 1 portion) 93
Succulent Lamb Shank (2 servings, serving: 1 portion) 94
Scrumptious Lamb Shank (4 servings, serving: 1 portion) 95
Festive Leg of Lamb (10 servings, serving: 1 portion) 96

Restaurant Style Leg of Lamb (6 servings, serving: 1 portion) 98

Luxurious Leg of Lamb (8 servings, serving: 1 portion) 99

Appetizing Lamb Shoulder (8 servings, serving: 1 portion) 100

Luscious Lamb Shoulder (8 servings, serving: 1 portion) 101

Simply Delicious Lamb Breast (2 servings, serving: 1 portion) 102

Best-Ever Flounder Parcel (2 servings, serving: 1 portion) 103

Crispy Trout (6 servings, serving: 1 portion) 104

Trout (8 servings, serving: 1 portion) 105

Lively flavored Trout (5 servings, serving: 1 portion) 106

Citrus Salmon (6 servings, serving: 1 portion) 107

Strengthening Salmon (6 servings, serving: 1 portion) 108

Omega-3 Rich Salmon (4 servings, serving: 1 portion) 109

Time Saving Dinner (4 servings, serving: 1 portion) 110

Nutritive Flounder (4 servings, serving: 1 portion) 111

Enjoyable Scallops (4 servings, serving: 1 portion) 112

Appealing Shrimp (8 servings, serving: 1 portion) 113

Lemony Shrimp (6 servings, serving: 1 portion) 114

Yummy Prawns Treat (3 servings, serving: 1 portion) 115

Perfectly Grilled Lobster Tails (4 servings, serving: 1 portion) 116

Super-Tasty Clams (6 servings, serving: 1 portion) 117

Satisfying Meatballs (6 servings, serving: 1 portion) 118

Texas Style Sausage Poppers (4 servings, serving: 1 portion) 120

Luncheon Turkey Burgers (4 servings, serving: 1 portion) 121

Flavorsome Cheeseburgers (4 servings, serving: 1 portion) 122

Earthy Flavored Meatloaf (20 servings, serving: 1 portion) 123

Great Meat Combo Loaf (10 servings, serving: 1 portion) 125

Nicely Charred Meatloaf (8 servings, serving: 1 portion) 126

Award Winning Pot Pie (10 servings, serving: 1 portion) 128

Mexican Stuffed Peppers (6 servings, serving: 1 portion) 129

- Fancy Party Time Treat (6 servings, serving: 1 portion) 130
- Comforting Casserole (8 servings, serving: 1 portion) 131
- Creamy Casserole (10 servings, serving: 1 portion) 132
- Classic Mac & Cheese (12 servings, serving: 1 portion) 134
- Cheesy Corn (12 servings, serving: 1 portion) 136
- Old-Fashioned Beans (16 servings, serving: 1 portion) 137
- Super-Fun Potatoes (6 servings, serving: 1 portion) 138
- Irish Bread (10 servings, serving: 1 portion) 139
- Southern Cornbread (8 servings, serving: 1 portion) 141
- Fall Time Apple Pie (8 servings, serving: 1 portion) 143
- Sweet Tooth Carving Crunch (8 servings, serving: 1 portion) 145
- Chocolate Lover's Cheesecake (8 servings, serving: 1 portion) 146
- Kid's Favorite Brownies (20 servings, serving: 1 portion) 148

Festive Whole Chicken (6 servings, serving: 1 portion)

Per Serving, Calories: 658- Fat: 22.8g - Carbs: 20.7g - Protein: 88.1g

Ingredients:

- ¾ cup dark brown sugar
- ½ cup ground espresso beans
- 1 tablespoon ground cumin
- 1 tablespoon ground cinnamon
- 1 tablespoon garlic powder
- 1 tablespoon cayenne pepper
- Salt and freshly ground black pepper, to taste
- 1 (4-pound) giblets removed whole chicken

Directions:

1. Preheat the pallet grill to 200-225 degrees F.
2. In a bowl, mix together all ingredients except chicken.
3. Rub the chicken with spice mixture generously.
4. Place the chicken in pallet grill and cook, covered for about 3-5 hours.
5. Remove chicken from pallet grill and transfer onto a cutting board for about 10 minutes before carving.
6. With a sharp knife, cut the chicken in desired sized pieces and serve.

Entrée Chicken (4 servings, serving: 1 portion)

Per Serving, Calories: 804- Fat: 25.3g - Carbs: 40.3g - Protein: 99.1g

Ingredients:

For Brine:

- 1 cup brown sugar
- ½ cup kosher salt
- 16 cups water

For Chicken:

- 1 (3-5-pound) whole chicken
- 1 tablespoon crushed garlic
- 1 teaspoon onion powder
- Salt and freshly ground black pepper, to taste
- 1 quartered medium yellow onion
- 3 peeled whole garlic cloves
- 1 quartered lemon
- 4-5 fresh thyme sprigs

Directions:

1. For brine: in a bucket, dissolve brown sugar and kosher salt in water. Place the chicken in brine and refrigerate overnight. Preheat the pallet grill to 225 degrees F. Remove the chicken from brine and with paper towels, pat it dry.

2. In a small bowl, mix together crushed garlic, onion powder, salt and black pepper. Rub chicken with garlic mixture evenly. Stuff the cavity of chicken with onion, garlic cloves, lemon and thyme.

3. With kitchen strings, tie the legs together. Place the chicken in pallet grill and cook, covered for about 2½-3 hours. Remove chicken from pallet grill and transfer onto a cutting board for about 10 minutes before carving.

4. With a sharp knife, cut the chicken in desired sized pieces and serve.

Christmas Dinner Chicken (4 servings, serving: 1 portion)

Per Serving, Calories: 1063- Fat: 49.4g - Carbs: 33.7g - Protein: 1116.1g

Ingredients:

- 1 (3-pound) whole chicken
- Salt and freshly ground black pepper, to taste
- 4 tablespoons butter, divided
- 1 chopped medium onion
- 4 chopped bacon strips
- 1 cup fresh mushrooms, sliced
- 1 cup wild rice mix
- 2¼ cups water
- 2 tablespoons chopped fresh parsley

Directions:

1. Remove the giblets of chicken and chop them roughly. Season chicken with salt and black pepper from inside and outside generously. In a large pan, melt 2 tablespoons of butter over medium heat and sauté onion for about 3-5 minutes.

2. Add bacon and cook till browned, stirring continuously. Add mushrooms, rice, salt and black pepper and stir to combine. Add water and bring to a boil. Reduce heat to low and simmer, covered for about 25 minutes or till all the liquid is absorbed. Stir in parsley and remove from heat. Preheat the pallet grill to 375 degrees F.

3. Stuff the cavity of chicken with rice mixture loosely. Tie chicken legs back with butcher's twine. With kitchen strings, tie the legs together. Place the chicken in pallet grill and cook for about 1¼ hours.

4. Remove chicken from pallet grill and transfer onto a cutting board for about 10 minutes before carving. With a sharp knife, cut the chicken in desired sized pieces and serve alongside stuffing.

Super-Tasty Chicken Drumsticks (6 servings, serving: 1 portion)

Per Serving, Calories: 385- Fat: 10.5g - Carbs: 22.7g - Protein: 47.6g

Ingredients:

- 1 cup fresh orange juice
- ¼ cup honey
- 2 tablespoons sweet chili sauce
- 2 tablespoons hoisin sauce
- 2 tablespoons finely grated fresh ginger
- 2 tablespoons minced garlic
- 1 teaspoon Sriracha
- ½ teaspoon sesame oil
- 6 chicken drumsticks

Directions:

1. Preheat the pallet grill to 225 degrees F. In a bowl, mix together all ingredients except chicken drumsticks.

2. Reserve half of honey mixture as a sauce. Coat the chicken drumsticks with remaining honey mixture.

3. Arrange the chicken drumsticks in pallet grill and cook for about 2 hours, coating with remaining honey mixture occasionally.

4. Serve drumsticks with reserved honey mixture as sauce.

Divine Chicken Drumsticks (8 servings, serving: 1 portion)

Per Serving, Calories: 319- Fat: 9.8g - Carbs: 7.7g - Protein: 46.8g

Ingredients:

- 8 chicken drumsticks
- Salt and freshly ground black pepper, to taste
- 6-ounce spicy BBQ sauce

Directions:

1. With kitchen shears, trim half of the top and bottom knuckle of each chicken drumstick to release the tendons and ligaments.

2. Season each drumstick with salt and black pepper generously and keep aside for about 20 minutes. Preheat the pallet grill to 275 degrees F.

3. Arrange the chicken drumsticks in pallet grill and cook for about 30 minutes per side. Remove drumsticks from the grate and place in a baking dish.

4. With a piece of foil, cover the baking dish and cook for about 45 minutes. Remove the foil and coat the drumsticks with BBQ sauce evenly. Cook for about 15 minutes more. Serve immediately.

Decadent Chicken Drumsticks (6 servings, serving: 1 portion)

Per Serving, Calories: 586- Fat: 43.7g - Carbs: 2.1g - Protein: 47.3g

Ingredients:

- 1 teaspoon dried thyme
- 1 tablespoon paprika
- 1 tablespoon cayenne pepper
- 1 teaspoon ground cumin
- 1 teaspoon garlic powder
- 1 teaspoon onion powder
- Salt and freshly ground black pepper, to taste
- 6 chicken drumsticks
- 1 cup olive oil

Directions

1. Preheat the pallet grill to 220 degrees F. In a bowl, mix together thyme, spices, salt and balk pepper.
2. Coat chicken drumsticks with oil generously and rub with spice mixture evenly.
3. Arrange the chicken drumsticks in pallet grill and cook for about 2 hours, flipping occasionally.

Drunken Drumsticks (8 servings, serving: 1 portion)

Per Serving, Calories: 601- Fat: 21.4g - Carbs: 27.6g - Protein: 63g

Ingredients:

For Brine:

- ½ cup brown sugar
- ½ cup kosher salt
- 5 cups water
- 2 (12-ounce) bottles beer
- 8 chicken drumsticks

For Coating:

- ¼ cup olive oil
- ½ cup BBQ rub
- 1 tablespoon minced fresh parsley
- 1 tablespoon minced fresh chives
- ¾ cup BBQ sauce
- ¼ cup beer

Directions:

1. For brine: in a bucket, dissolve brown sugar and kosher salt in water and beer. Place the chicken drumsticks in brine and refrigerate, covered for about 3 hours. Preheat the pallet grill to 275 degrees F.
2. Remove chicken drumsticks from brine and rinse under cold running water. With paper towels, pat dry chicken drumsticks. Coat drumsticks with olive oil and rub with BBQ rub evenly.
3. Sprinkle drumsticks with parsley and chives. Arrange the chicken drumsticks in pallet grill and cook for about 45 minutes. Meanwhile, in a bowl, mix together BBQ sauce and beer.
4. Remove from grill and coat the drumsticks with BBQ sauce evenly. Cook for about 15 minutes more. Serve immediately.

Super-Easy Chicken Quarters (8 servings, serving: 1 portion)

Per Serving, Calories: 485- Fat: 23.1g - Carbs: 0g - Protein: 65.6g

Ingredients:

- 8 connected chicken legs and thighs quartered
- ¼ cup olive oil
- ½ cup poultry rub

Directions:

1. With paper towels, pat dry chicken quarters.
2. In a large bowl, add all ingredients and coat chicken quarters with oil and rub generously. Refrigerate, covered for at least 2 hours.
3. Preheat the pallet grill on Smoke with the lid open for about 4-5 minutes. Arrange the chicken drumsticks in pallet grill and cook for about 1 hour.
4. Now, set the pallet grill to 350 degrees F and cook for about 50-60 minutes. Serve immediately.

Awesome Chicken Quarters (6 servings, serving: 1 portion)

Per Serving, Calories: 579- Fat: 23.4g - Carbs: 23g - Protein: 55.9g

Ingredients:

For Brine:

- 1 cup kosher salt
- ¾ cup light brown sugar
- 16 cups water
- 6 connected chicken legs and thighs quartered

For Mayo Glaze:

- ½ cup mayonnaise
- 2 tablespoons BBQ rub
- 2 tablespoons minced fresh chives
- 1 tablespoon minced garlic

Directions:

1. For brine: in a bucket, dissolve salt and brown sugar in water. Place the chicken quarters in brine and refrigerate, covered for about 4 hours.

2. Remove chicken quarters from brine and rinse under cold running water. With paper towels, pat dry chicken quarters. For mayo glaze: in a bowl, add all ingredients and mix till ell combined.

3. Coat chicken quarters with glaze evenly. Preheat the pallet grill to 275 degrees F. Arrange the chicken drumsticks in pallet grill and cook for about 1-1½ hours.

4. Serve immediately.

Juicy Chicken Thighs (6 servings, serving: 1 portion)

Per Serving, Calories: 323- Fat: 12.6g - Carbs: 0g - Protein: 49.2g

Ingredients:

- 6 trimmed bone-in, skin-on chicken thighs
- Salt and freshly ground black pepper, to taste
- 8-ounce chicken rub

Directions:

1. Preheat the pallet grill to 350 degrees F.
2. Season chicken thighs with salt and black pepper lightly and then, coat with chicken rub.
3. Arrange the chicken drumsticks in pallet grill and cook for about 35 minutes.
4. Serve immediately.

Flavorsome Chicken Thighs (4 servings, serving: 1 portion)

Per Serving, Calories: 455- Fat: 19.7g - Carbs: 18.8g - Protein: 49.9g

Ingredients:

- 2 minced garlic cloves
- ¼ cup honey
- 2 tablespoons soy sauce
- ¼ teaspoon crushed red pepper flakes
- 4 skinless, boneless chicken thighs
- 2 tablespoons olive oil
- 2 teaspoons sweet rub
- ¼ teaspoon red chili powder
- ¼ teaspoon freshly ground black pepper

Directions:

1. Preheat the pallet grill to 400 degrees F.
2. In a small bowl, add garlic, honey, soy sauce and red pepper flakes and with a wire whisk, beat till well combined.
3. Coat chicken thighs with oil and season with sweet rub, chili powder and black pepper generously.
4. Arrange the chicken drumsticks in pallet grill and cook for about 15 minutes per In the last 4-5 minutes of cooking, coat drumsticks with garlic mixture.
5. Serve immediately.

Luscious Chicken Breasts (6 servings, serving: 1 portion)

Per Serving, Calories: 1161- Fat: 49.6g - Carbs: 92.2g - Protein: 81.4g

Ingredients:

For Brine:

- ¼ cup brown sugar
- ¼ cup kosher salt
- 4 cups water

For Chicken:

- 6 skinless, boneless chicken breasts
- ¼ cup chicken rub
- 18 bacon slices
- 1½ cups BBQ sauce

Directions:

For brine: in a pitcher, dissolve sugar and salt in water. Place the chicken breasts in brine and refrigerate for about 2 hours, flipping once in the middle way.

Preheat the pallet grill to 230 degrees F. Remove chicken breasts from brine and rinse under cold running water.

Season chicken breasts with rub generously. Arrange 3 bacon strips of bacon onto a cutting board, against each other. Place 1 chicken breast across the bacon, leaving enough bacon on the left side to wrap it over just a little.

Wrap the bacon strips around chicken breast and secure with toothpicks. Repeat with remaining breasts and bacon slices.

Arrange the chicken breasts into pallet grill and cook for about 2½ hours.

Coat the breasts with BBQ sauce and cook for about 30 minutes. Serve immediately.

Weeknight Chicken Breasts (6 servings, serving: 1 portion)

Per Serving, Calories: 350- Fat: 11.3g - Carbs: 15.1g - Protein: 43.8g

Ingredients:

- 2 pound trimmed skinless, boneless chicken breasts
- 2 tablespoons Cajun seasoning
- 1 cup BBQ sauce

Directions:

1. Preheat the pallet grill to 225 degrees F.
2. Rub the chicken breasts with Cajun seasoning generously.
3. Arrange the chicken breasts into pallet grill and cook for about 4-6 hours.
4. During last hour of cooking, coat the breasts with BBQ sauce twice.

Exotic Chicken Breasts (4 servings, serving: 1 portion)

Per Serving, Calories: 475- Fat: 25.3g - Carbs: 9.6g - Protein: 49.4g

Ingredients:

- 1 teaspoon crushed garlic
- ¼ cup olive oil
- 1 tablespoon Worcestershire sauce
- 1 tablespoon sweet mesquite seasoning
- 4 chicken breasts
- 2 tablespoons regular BBQ sauce
- 2 tablespoons spicy BBQ sauce
- 2 tablespoons honey bourbon BBQ sauce

Directions:

1. Preheat the pallet grill to 450 degrees F.
2. In a large bowl, mix together gallic, oil, Worcestershire sauce and mesquite seasoning.
3. Coat chicken breasts with seasoning mixture evenly. Place the chicken breasts into pallet grill and cook for about 20-30 minutes.
4. Meanwhile, in a bowl, mix together all 3 BBQ sauces. In the last 4-5 minutes of cooking, coat breast with BBQ sauce mixture.
5. Serve immediately.

Flavored Chicken Wings (4 servings, serving: 1 portion)

Per Serving, Calories: 561- Fat: 17.8g - Carbs: 21.1g - Protein: 66.5g

Ingredients:

- ¾ cup BBQ sauce
- ¼ cup whiskey
- 1 tablespoon sugar
- 1/3 cup Dijon mustard
- 24 chicken wings
- Salt and freshly ground black pepper, to taste

Directions:

1. In a small pan, mix together BBQ sauce, whiskey and sugar on medium-high heat and bring to a boil.
2. Remove from heat and immediately, stir in Dijon mustard. Keep aside to cool completely.
3. Meanwhile with a sharp knife, cut each wing through the joints to separate the drumette.
4. Sprinkle the wings with salt and black pepper generously. In a sealable bag, add chicken wings and sauce.
5. Seal the bag and shake to coat well and refrigerate overnight.
6. Preheat the pallet grill to 250 degrees F. Remove the wings from bag and discard any excess marinade.
7. Arrange the wings in a large shallow aluminum pan in a single layer. Place the pan in pallet grill and cook for about 2 hours.

Asian Inspired Chicken Wings (4 servings, serving: 1 portion)

Per Serving, Calories: 508- Fat: 19.6g - Carbs: 12.4g - Protein: 67.2g

Ingredients:

- 2 pound chicken wings
- 2 crushed garlic cloves
- 3 tablespoons hoisin sauce
- 2 tablespoons soy sauce
- 1 teaspoon dark sesame oil
- 1 tablespoon honey
- ½ teaspoon ginger powder
- 1 tablespoon lightly toasted sesame seeds

Directions:

1. Preheat the pallet grill to 225 degrees F.
2. Arrange the wings onto the lower rack of pallet grill and cook for about 1½ hours.
3. Meanwhile, in a large bowl, mix together remaining all ingredients. Remove wings from pallet grill and place in the bowl of garlic mixture.
4. Coat wings with garlic mixture generously. Now, set the pallet grill to 375 degrees F. Arrange coated wings onto a foil lined baking sheet and sprinkle with sesame seeds.
5. Place the pan onto the lower rack of pallet grill and cook, covered for about 25-30 minutes.
6. Serve immediately.

Summertime Dinner Hens (4 servings, serving: 1 portion)

Per Serving, Calories: 311- Fat: 25.9g - Carbs: 1.1g - Protein: 17g

Ingredients:

- 4 Cornish game hens
- 4 fresh rosemary sprigs
- 4 tablespoons melted butter
- 4 teaspoons chicken rub

Directions:

1. Preheat the pallet grill to 375 degrees F.
2. With paper towels, pat dry hens.
3. Tuck the wings behind the backs and with kitchen strings, tie the legs together.
4. Coat the outside of each hen with melted butter and sprinkle with rub evenly.
5. Stuff the cavity of each hen with a rosemary sprig.
6. Place the hens in pallet grill and cook for about 50-60 minutes.
7. Remove the hens from pallet grill and transfer onto a platter for about 5 minutes before serving.

Favorite Whole Turkey (16 servings, serving: 1 portion)

Per Serving, Calories: 761- Fat: 14.5g - Carbs: 2.3g - Protein: 124.9g

Ingredients:

- 1 (15-pound) neck and giblets removed whole turkey
- ¼ cup olive oil
- Salt and freshly ground black pepper, to taste
- 1 cup chicken broth
- 2 tablespoons apple cider vinegar
- 2 tablespoons honey

Directions:

1. Preheat the pallet grill to 275 degrees F.
2. Arrange a rack in a large roasting pan. Place turkey over rack in roasting pan.
3. Coat the turkey with oil generously and then season with salt and black pepper evenly.
4. Place the roasting pan in pallet grill and cook for about 45 minutes. Meanwhile in a bowl, mix together remaining ingredients.
5. After 45 minutes, coat the turkey with honey mixture. Cook for about 3½-4½ hours, coating with honey mixture after every 45 minutes.
6. Remove turkey from pallet grill and transfer onto a cutting board for about 15-20 minutes before carving.
7. With a sharp knife, cut the turkey in desired sized pieces and serve.

Thanksgiving Turkey (12 servings, serving: 1 portion)

Per Serving, Calories: 729- Fat: 25.6g - Carbs: 8.1g - Protein: 52g

Ingredients:

- 1 cored and quartered apple
- 1 quartered onion
- ½ cup softened butter
- Salt and freshly ground black pepper, to taste
- 4 crushed garlic cloves
- 1 (10-pound) neck and giblets removed whole turkey
- 2 tablespoons seasoned salt

Directions:

1. Preheat the pallet grill to 225-250 degrees F.
2. For stuffing in a bowl, mix together apple, onion, butter, salt and black pepper.
3. Rub the crushed garlic over the outer side of turkey evenly and then, sprinkle with seasoned salt. Stuff the cavity of turkey with apple mixture.
4. Arrange the turkey in a disposable roasting pan and with a piece of foil, cover the roasting pan loosely.
5. Place the roasting pan in pallet grill and cook for about 10 minutes, basting with pan juices after every 1 hour.
6. Remove turkey from pallet grill and transfer onto a cutting board for about 15-20 minutes before carving.
7. With a sharp knife, cut the turkey in desired sized pieces and serve.

Family Dinner Turkey (16 servings, serving: 1 portion)

Per Serving, Calories: 867- Fat: 36.6g - Carbs: 1.8g - Protein: 125.3g

Ingredients:

- 1 (15-pound) neck and giblets removed whole turkey
- 1 cup butter
- ¼ cup olive oil
- 6-8 chopped jalapeño peppers
- ½ minced red onion
- 2 tablespoons minced garlic
- 1 cup chicken broth
- Butter flavored cooking spray
- 2 tablespoons Italian seasoning
- 1 tablespoon granulated garlic

Directions:

1. Preheat the pallet grill to 200 degrees F. In a large pan, add butter, oil, jalapeños, onion and garlic on medium-high heat and cook for about 4-5 minutes.

2. Add broth and bring to a boil. Boil for about 5 minutes. Through a strainer, strain mixture into a bowl and discard the solids.

3. With a baster-injector, inject turkey all over with strained liquid. Spray the outside of turkey with cooking spray and season with Italian seasoning and garlic. Arrange the turkey in pallet grill and cook for about 30 minutes.

4. Remove turkey from pallet grill and again, inject with strained liquid. Now, set the pallet grill to 325 degrees F. Cook for about 2½-3 hours.

5. Remove turkey from pallet grill and transfer onto a cutting board for about 15-20 minutes before carving. With a sharp knife, cut the turkey in desired sized pieces and serve.

Simplest Turkey Breast (12 servings, serving: 1 portion)

Per Serving, Calories: 363- Fat: 12.3g - Carbs: 16g - Protein: 45.3g

Ingredients:

For Brine:

- ¾ cup kosher salt
- 1/3 cup brown sugar
- 16 cups water
- 1 (7-pound) trimmed skin-on, bone-in turkey breast

For Herb Butter:

- 8 tablespoons softened butter
- ¼ cup chopped mixed fresh herbs (rosemary, sage, marjoram and parsley)
- 1 minced garlic clove
- 1 teaspoon grated fresh lemon zest
- 1 tablespoon fresh lemon juice
- Salt and freshly ground black pepper, to taste

Directions:

In a large pan, dissolve salt and brown sugar in water. Place the turkey breast in brine and refrigerate for about 6-8 hours or overnight. Preheat the pallet grill to 200 degrees F.

Drain the turkey breast and with paper towels, pat dry completely. Place the turkey breast onto a rack arranged in a shallow roasting pan. Carefully, add 1 cup of water in the bottom of roasting pan.

For herb butter: in a bowl, add butter, herbs, garlic, lemon zest, lemon juice, salt and black pepper and mix well. Remove from microwave and stir to combine. With your fingers, carefully loosen the skin of breast.

Rub about 2 tablespoons of herb butter under the skin on each side of the breastbone evenly. In a microwave-safe bowl, add 4 tablespoons of butter mixture and microwave on Medium-Low till melted completely.

Coat the outside of turkey breast with some melted butter. Arrange the turkey in pallet grill and cook for about 2-2½ hours, coating with remaining butter mixture once after 1½ hours. Remove turkey breast from pallet grill and transfer onto a cutting board for about 15 minutes before slicing.

With a sharp knife, cut the turkey in desired sized slices and serve.

Glazed Turkey Breast (6 servings, serving: 1 portion)

Per Serving, Calories: 387- Fat: 6.4g - Carbs: 34.8g - Protein: 45.3g

Ingredients:

- ½ cup honey
- ¼ cup dry sherry
- 1 tablespoon butter
- 2 tablespoons fresh lemon juice
- Salt, to taste
- 1 (3-3½-pound) skinless, boneless turkey breast

Directions:

1. In a small pan, mix together honey, sherry and butter on low heat and cook, stirring continuously till the mixture becomes smooth.
2. Remove from heat and stir in lemon juice and salt.
3. Keep aside to cool. Transfer the honey mixture and turkey breast in a sealable bag.
4. Seal the bag and shake to coat evenly. Refrigerate for about 6-10 hours.
5. Preheat the pellet grill to 225-250 degrees F.
6. Place the turkey breast in pallet grill and cook for about 2½-4 hours or till desired doneness.

Sunday Dinner Turkey Legs (6 servings, serving: 1 portion)

Per Serving, Calories: 1061 Fat: 54g - Carbs: 4.9g - Protein: 127.8g

Ingredients:

For Turkey:

- 3 tablespoons Worcestershire sauce
- 1 tablespoon canola oil
- 6 turkey legs

For Rub:

- ¼ cup chipotle seasoning
- 1 tablespoon brown sugar
- 1 tablespoon paprika

For Sauce:

- 1 cup white vinegar
- 1 tablespoon canola oil
- 1 tablespoon chipotle BBQ sauce

Directions:

For turkey in a bowl, mix together Worcestershire sauce and canola oil. With your fingers, loosen the skin of legs.

With your fingers coat the legs under the skin with oil mixture. In another bowl, mix together rub ingredients. Rub the spice mixture under and outer surface of turkey legs generously.

Transfer the legs into a large sealable bag and refrigerate for about 2-4 hours. Remove the turkey legs from refrigerator and keep at room temperature for at least 30 minutes before cooking. Preheat the pallet grill to 200-220 degrees F.

In a small pan, mix together all sauce ingredients on low heat and cook till warmed completely, stirring continuously. Place the turkey legs in the pallet grill cook for about 3½-4 hours, coating with sauce after every 45 minutes.

Standard Turkey Legs (4 servings, serving: 1 portion)

Per Serving, Calories: 432- Fat: 8g - Carbs: 19.9g - Protein: 67.2g

Ingredients:

- 16 cups warm water
- 1 cup BBQ rub
- ½ cup brown sugar
- ½ cup curing salt
- 2 bay leaves
- 1 tablespoon whole peppercorns
- 1 tablespoon crushed allspice berries
- 2 teaspoons liquid smoke
- 8 cups cold water
- 4 cups ice
- 4 turkey legs

Directions:

1. In a large pan, add all ingredients except cold water, ice and turkey legs on high heat and bring to a boil, stirring continuously to dissolve the salt granules.

2. Remove from heat and keep aside at room temperature to cool. Add cold water and ice and refrigerator to chill. Add the turkey legs and refrigerate for about 24 hours.

3. Preheat the pallet grill to 250 degrees F. Remove turkey legs from brine and rinse under running cold water.

4. With paper towels, pat dry turkey legs completely. Place the turkey legs directly on the grill grate and cook for about 4-5 hours.

Simply Perfect Duck (6 servings, serving: 1 portion)

Per Serving, Calories: 789- Fat: 42.8g - Carbs: 6.9g - Protein: 89.4g

Ingredients:

- 1 (5-6-pound) giblets removed and trimmed whole duck
- ½ cup pork & poultry rub
- 1 quartered orange
- 1 quartered small onion
- ¼ cup chopped fresh rosemary

Directions:

Preheat the pallet grill to 325 degrees F.

Wash the duck under cold running water completely and with paper towels, pat dry it.

With the tip of a knife, prick the skin all over the duck.

Season the duck with rub generously.

Stuff the cavity of duck with orange, onion and rosemary and then, tie the legs together with kitchen strings.

Arrange the duck directly on the grill grate and cook for about 2½-3 hours.

Remove duck from pallet grill and transfer onto a cutting board for about 15 minutes before carving.

With a sharp knife, cut the duck in desired sized pieces and serve.

Crispy Duck (6 servings, serving: 1 portion)

Per Serving, Calories: 942- Fat: 42.4g - Carbs: 41.1g - Protein: 91.5g

Ingredients:

- ¾ cup honey
- ¾ cup soy sauce
- ¾ cup red wine
- 2 tablespoons black pepper
- 1½ tablespoons garlic salt
- 1 (5-pound) giblets removed and trimmed whole duck

Directions:

1. Preheat the pallet grill to 225-250 degrees F.
2. In a bowl, add all ingredients except duck and mix till well combined.
3. With a fork, poke holes in the skin of the duck.
4. Coat the duck with honey mixture generously.
5. Arrange duck in pallet gill, breast side down and cook for about 4 hours, coating with honey mixture one after 2 hours.
6. Remove duck from pallet grill and transfer onto a cutting board for about 15 minutes before carving.
7. With a sharp knife, cut the duck in desired sized pieces and serve.

2 ingredients Dinner (4 servings, serving: 1 portion)

Per Serving, Calories: 219- Fat: 6.8g - Carbs: 0g - Protein: 37.4g

Ingredients:

- 4 (6-ounce) boneless duck breasts
- ¼ cup chicken rub

Directions:

1. Preheat the pallet grill to 275 degrees F.
2. With a sharp knife, score the skin of the duck into ¼-inch diamond pattern.
3. Season the duck breast with rub evenly.
Arrange the duck breasts in the pallet grill, meat side down and cook for about 10 minutes.
4. Set the pallet grill to 400 degrees F.
5. Now, arrange the breasts in the pallet grill, skin side down and cook for about 10 minutes.
6. Remove turkey from pallet grill and transfer duck breast onto a cutting board for about 5 minutes before carving.
7. With a sharp knife, cut the duck breast against the grain in thick slices and serve.

Irresistible Duck Legs (8 servings, serving: 1 portion)

Per Serving, Calories: 353- Fat: 10.3g - Carbs: 12.9g - Protein: 49.7g

Ingredients:

For Glaze:

- ¼ cup fresh orange juice
- ¼ cup orange marmalade
- ¼ cup mirin
- 2 tablespoons hoisin sauce
- ½ teaspoon crushed red pepper flakes

For Duck Rub:

- 1 teaspoons kosher salt
- ¾ teaspoon freshly ground black pepper
- ¾ teaspoon Chinese five spice powder
- 8 (6-ounce) trimmed duck legs

Directions:

1. Preheat the pallet grill to 235 degrees F.
2. Forb glaze: in a small pan, add all ingredients on medium-high heat and bring to gentle boil, stirring continuously. Remove from heat and keep aside.
3. For rub: in a small bowl, mix together salt, black pepper and 5 spice powder.
4. Rub the duck legs with spice rub evenly.
5. Arrange the duck legs in on the grill, skin side up and cook for about 50 minutes.
6. Coat the duck legs with glaze ad cook for about 20 minutes, flipping and coating with glaze after every 5 minutes.

Fancy Dinner Goose (12 servings, serving: 1 portion)

Per Serving, Calories: 905- Fat: 60.2g - Carbs: 23g - Protein: 63.2g

Ingredients:

- 1½ cups kosher salt
- 1 cup brown sugar
- 20 cups water
- 1 (12-pound) giblets removed whole goose
- 1 cut into 6 wedges 1 naval orange
- 1 cut into 8 wedges large onion
- 2 bay leaves
- ¼ cup crushed juniper berries
- 12 black peppercorns
- Salt and freshly ground black pepper, to taste
- 1 cut into 6 wedges 1 apple
- 2-3 fresh parsley sprigs

Directions:

1. Trim off any loose neck skin. Trim the first two joints off the wings. Wash the goose under cold running water and with paper towels, pat dry it.

2. With the tip of a paring knife, prick the goose all over the skin. In a large pitcher, dissolve kosher salt and brown sugar in water.

3. Squeeze 3 orange wedges into brine. Add goose, 4 onion wedges, bay leaves, juniper berries and peppercorns in brine and refrigerate for 24 hours.

4. Preheat the pallet grill to 350 degrees F. Remove the goose from brine and with paper towels, pat dry completely. Season the goose, inside and out with salt and black pepper evenly.

5. Stuff the cavity with apple wedges, herbs, remaining orange and onion wedges. With kitchen strings, tie the legs together loosely. Place the goose onto a rack arranged in a shallow roasting pan.

6. Arrange the goose in the pallet grill and cook for about 1 hour. With a basting bulb, remove some of the fat from the pan and cook for about 1 hour. Again, remove excess fat from the pan and cook for about ½-1 hour more. Remove goose from pallet grill and transfer onto a cutting board for about 20 minutes before carving.

7. With a sharp knife, cut the goose in desired sized pieces and serve.

Sweet & Tangy Goose Breast (8 servings, serving: 1 portion)

Per Serving, Calories: 285- Fat: 13.4g - Carbs: 17.8g - Protein: 27.5g

Ingredients:

- ½ cup fresh orange juice
- 1/3 cup olive oil
- 1/3 cup brown sugar
- 1/3 cup Dijon mustard
- ¼ cup honey
- ¼ cup soy sauce
- 1 tablespoon dried minced onion
- 1 teaspoon garlic powder
- 8 goose breast halves

Directions:

1. In a large bowl, add all ingredients except goose breast and beat till well combined.
2. Add goose breast halves and coat with marinade generously. Refrigerate, covered for about 3-6 hours.
3. Preheat the pallet grill to 300 degrees F.
4. Remove goose breasts from bowl, reserving marinade.
5. Arrange the goose breasts in the pallet grill and cook for about 30 minutes, coating with reserve marinade occasionally.
6. Now, cook for about 10-15 minutes more.

Succulent Beef Tenderloin (12 servings, serving: 1 portion)

Per Serving, Calories: 425- Fat: 21.5g - Carbs: 0g - Protein: 54.7g

Ingredients:

- 1 (5-pound) trimmed beef tenderloin
- Kosher salt, to taste
- ¼ cup olive oil
- Freshly ground black pepper, to taste

Directions:

1. With kitchen strings, tie the tenderloin in 7-8 places.
2. Season tenderloin with kosher salt generously.
3. With a plastic wrap, cover the tenderloin and keep aside at room temperature for about 1 hour.
4. Preheat the pellet grill to 225-250 degrees F.
5. Now, coat tenderloin with oil evenly and season with black pepper.
6. Arrange tenderloin in the pallet grill and cook for about 55-65 minutes.
7. Now, place cooking grate directly over hot coals and sear tenderloin for about 2 minutes per side.
8. Transfer the tenderloin onto a cutting board and keep aside for about 10-15 minutes before serving.
9. With a sharp knife, cut the tenderloin in desired sized slices and serve.

Versatile Beef Tenderloin (6 servings, serving: 1 portion)

Per Serving, Calories: 493- Fat: 29.2g - Carbs: 3.4g - Protein: 44.3g

Ingredients:

For Brandy Butter:

- ½ cup melted butter
- 1-ounce brandy

For Brandy Sauce:

- 2-ounce brandy
- 8 minced garlic cloves
- ¼ cup chopped mixed fresh herbs (parsley, rosemary and thyme)
- 2 teaspoons honey
- 2 teaspoons hot English mustard

For Tenderloin:

- 1 (2-pound) center-cut beef tenderloin
- Salt and cracked black peppercorns, to taste

Directions:

Preheat the pellet grill to 230 degrees F.

For butter injection: in a pan, melt butter on medium-low heat. Stir in brandy and remove from heat. Keep side, covered to keep warm. For mustard sauce: in a bowl, add all ingredients and mix till well combined. Season tenderloin with salt and black peppercorns generously. Coat tenderloin with mustard sauce evenly.

With a baster-injector, inject tenderloin with brandy butter. Arrange tenderloin in the pallet grill and cook for about ½-2 hours, injecting with brandy butter occasionally.

Transfer the tenderloin onto a cutting board and keep aside for about 10-15 minutes before serving. With a sharp knife, cut the tenderloin in desired sized slices and serve.

Delish Rib Roast (10 servings, serving: 1 portion)

Per Serving, Calories: 490- Fat: 21.3g - Carbs: 1.9g - Protein: 69.1g

Ingredients:

- 1 (5-pound) boneless prime rib roast
- Salt, to taste
- 5 tablespoons olive oil
- 2 tablespoons cracked black pepper
- 2 teaspoons crushed dried thyme
- 2 teaspoons crushed dried rosemary
- 2 teaspoons garlic powder
- 1 teaspoon onion powder
- 1 teaspoon paprika
- ½ teaspoon cayenne pepper

Directions:

1. Season the roast with salt generously. With a plastic wrap, cover the roast and refrigerate for about 24 hours. In a bowl, mix together remaining ingredients and keep aside for about 1 hour. Massage the roast with oil mixture evenly. Arrange the roast in a large plate and refrigerate for about 6-12 hours. Soak pecan wood chips in water for at least 1 hour.

2. Preheat the pellet grill to 225-230 degrees F.

3. Arrange roast in the pallet grill and cook for about 3-3½ hours. Meanwhile preheat the oven to 500 degrees F. Remove roast from pallet grill and transfer onto a large baking sheet. Roast for about 15-20 minutes.

4. Remove the roast from oven and transfer onto a cutting board for about 10-15 minutes before slicing. With a sharp knife, cut the roast in desired sized slices and serve.

Aromatic Rib Roast (12 servings, serving: 1 portion)

Per Serving, Calories: 358- Fat: 19.8g - Carbs: 0.9g - Protein: 42.7g

Ingredients:

- 3 tablespoons olive oil
- 2 tablespoons minced flat-leaf parsley
- 2 tablespoons minced thyme leaves
- 2 tablespoons minced tarragon
- 2 tablespoons minced rosemary leaves
- 1 tablespoon minced garlic
- Sea salt and freshly ground black pepper, to taste
- ¼ teaspoon crushed red pepper flakes
- 1 (6-pound) trimmed boneless prime rib roast

Directions:

1. Preheat the pellet grill to 325 degrees F by starting the fire on one side.
2. In a large bowl, add all ingredients except rib roast and mix till well combined.
3. Coat rib roast with herb mixture generously.
4. Arrange the rib roast in pellet grill on the side away from fire and cook, covered for about 1-1½ hours.
5. Remove the roast from oven and transfer onto a cutting board for about 15-20 minutes before slicing.
6. With a sharp knife, cut the roast in desired sized slices and serve.

Simply Tasty Roast (8 servings, serving: 1 portion)

Per Serving, Calories: 322- Fat: 10.6g - Carbs: 1.4g - Protein: 51.9g

Ingredients:

- 1 tablespoon granulated onion
- 1 tablespoon granulated garlic
- salt and freshly ground black pepper, to taste
- 1 (3-pound) trimmed tri tip roast

Directions:

1. In a bowl, mix together all ingredients except roast.
2. Coat roast with spice mixture generously.
3. Keep aside at room temperature till grill heats.
4. Preheat the pellet grill to 250 degrees F.
5. Arrange roast in the pallet grill and cook for about 25 minutes.
6. Now, set the grill to 350-400 degrees F and sear roast for about 3-4 minutes per side.
7. Remove the roast from oven and transfer onto a cutting board for about 15-20 minutes before slicing.
8. With a sharp knife, cut the roast across the grain into slices and serve.

Special Dinner Roast (8 servings, serving: 1 portion)

Per Serving, Calories: 408- Fat: 19.8g - Carbs: 2.2g - Protein: 52.1g

Ingredients:

For Roast Rub:

- 1½ teaspoons granulated garlic
- 1½ teaspoons granulated onion
- 1½ teaspoons paprika
- 1 teaspoon crushed dried rosemary
- ¼ teaspoon cayenne pepper
- Salt and freshly ground black pepper, to taste
- 1 (3-pound) trimmed tri tip roast

For Coating:

- 4 crushed garlic cloves
- 1/3 cup vegetable oil
- 1/3 cup red wine vinegar
- ½ tsp teaspoon Dijon mustard

Directions:

1. For roast rub: in a bowl, mix together all ingredients except roast. Rub roast with spice mixture generously. Arrange roast in a baking dish and refrigerate, covered for at least 4 hours.
2. Mix the vinegar, vegetable oil, crushed garlic and Dijon mustard together. Remove roast from refrigerator and keep aside at room temperature, uncovered for about 30-45 minutes before cooking.
3. Preheat the pellet grill to 400 degrees F. For coating: in a bowl, add all ingredients and mix till well combined. Coat roast with oil mixture evenly. Arrange roast in the pallet grill and cook for about 25-30 minutes, flipping and coating with oil mixture after every 5 minutes.
4. Remove the roast from oven and transfer onto a cutting board for about 15-20 minutes before slicing. With a sharp knife, cut the roast across the grain into slices and serve.

Stunning Rump Roast (8 servings, serving: 1 portion)

Per Serving, Calories: 248- Fat: 9.1g - Carbs: 1.4g - Protein: 37.8g

Ingredients:

- 1 teaspoon smoked paprika
- 1 teaspoon onion powder
- 1 teaspoon garlic powder
- Salt and freshly ground black pepper, to taste
- 3 pound beef rump roast
- 2 tablespoons Worcestershire sauce

Directions:

1. Preheat the pallet grill to 200 degrees F.
2. In a bowl, mix together all spices.
3. Coat the rump roast with Worcestershire sauce evenly and then rub with spice mixture generously.
4. Arrange the rump roast in pallet grill and cook for about 5-6 hours.
5. Remove the roast from the pallet grill and transfer onto a cutting board for about 10-15 minutes before slicing.
6. With a sharp knife, cut the roast in desired sized slices and serve.

Deliciously Spicy Roast (6 servings, serving: 1 portion)

Per Serving, Calories: 528- Fat: 19.7g - Carbs: 5.7g - Protein: 77.4g

Ingredients:

- 2 tablespoons onion powder
- 2 tablespoons garlic powder
- 2 tablespoons red chili powder
- ½ teaspoon crushed dried oregano
- ½ teaspoon crushed dried parsley
- Salt and freshly ground black pepper, to taste
- 1 (3 pound) chuck roast
- 16-ounce warm beef broth

Directions:

1. Preheat the pallet grill to 250 degrees F.
2. In a bowl, mix together all spices. Coat roast with spice mixture evenly.
3. Arrange the rump roast in pallet grill and cook for about 1½ hours per side.
4. Now, arrange chuck roast in a steaming pan with beef broth. With a piece of foil, cover the pan and cook for about 2-3 hours.
5. Remove the roast from the pallet grill and transfer onto a cutting board for about 30 minutes before slicing.
6. With a sharp knife, cut the roast in desired sized slices and serve.

Simple-Ever Chuck Roast (12 servings, serving: 1 portion)

Per Serving, Calories: 353- Fat:11.8g - Carbs: 0.5g - Protein: 57.4g

Ingredients:

- ¼ cup kosher salt
- ¼ cup freshly ground black pepper
- 1 (4-5-pound) beef chuck roll

Directions:

1. Preheat the pallet grill to 275-300 degrees F.
2. In a small bowl, mix together salt and black pepper.
3. Rub chuck roast with salt mixture generously. With kitchen twine, tie chuck roll around its circumference at 1-1½-inch intervals.
4. Arrange chuck roll in the pallet grill and cook for about 4 hours.
5. Remove chuck roll from the pallet grill and wrap with a piece of foil.
6. Now, set the pallet grill to 225-250 degrees F. Arrange chuck roll onto the cooler side of grill and cook for about 5-5½ hours.
7. Now, remove foil and cook for about 30 minutes more. Remove the roast from the pallet grill and transfer onto a cutting board for about 30 minutes before slicing.
8. With a sharp knife, cut the chuck roll in desired sized slices and serve.

Midweek Dinner Brisket (8 servings, serving: 1 portion)

Per Serving, Calories: 763- Fat: 23.1g - Carbs: 31g - Protein: 106.1g

Ingredients:

- 1 cup paprika
- ¾ cup sugar
- 3 tablespoons garlic salt
- 3 tablespoons onion powder
- 1 tablespoon celery salt
- 1 tablespoon lemon pepper
- 1 tablespoon freshly ground black pepper
- 1 teaspoon cayenne pepper
- 1 teaspoon mustard powder
- ½ teaspoon crushed dried thyme
- 1 (5-6-pound) trimmed beef brisket

Directions:

1. In a bowl, mix together all ingredients except beef brisket.
2. Rub the brisket with spice mixture generously. With a plastic wrap, cover the brisket and refrigerate overnight.
3. Preheat the pallet grill to 250 degrees F.
4. Arrange the brisket in pallet grill over indirect heat and cook for about 3-3½ hours. Flip and cook for about 3-3½ hours more.
5. Remove the brisket from pallet grill and transfer onto a cutting board for about 10-15 minutes before slicing. With a sharp knife, cut the brisket in desired sized slices and serve.

BBQ Party Brisket (12 servings, serving: 1 portion)

Per Serving, Calories: 593- Fat: 19.3g - Carbs: 4.4g - Protein: 92.2g

Ingredients:

For Dry Rub:

- 2 tablespoons brown sugar
- 2 tablespoons red chili powder
- 2 tablespoons paprika
- 2 tablespoons crushed red pepper flakes
- 1 teaspoon cayenne pepper
- 1 teaspoon ground cumin
- 1 teaspoon minced dried onion
- Salt and freshly ground black pepper, to taste

For Brisket:

- 1 (8-pound) beef brisket

For Coating:

- 1 can beer
- 1 cup apple cider vinegar
- 1 tablespoon brown sugar
- 2-3 minced garlic cloves
- 1 tablespoon crushed red pepper flakes

Directions:

1. For dry rub: in a bowl, mix together all ingredients.

2. Coat the brisket with dry rub generously and keep aside at room temperature for some time.

3. Preheat the pallet grill to 250 degrees F.

4. For coating mixture: in a bowl, add all ingredients and beat till well combined.

5. Arrange the brisket in pallet grill and cook for about 4 hours, coating with mixture after every 45 minutes.

6. Remove the brisket from pallet grill and transfer onto a cutting board for about 10-15 minutes before slicing.

7. With a sharp knife, cut the brisket in desired sized slices and serve.

Easy-to-Prepare Brisket (14 servings, serving: 1 portion)

Per Serving, Calories: 731- Fat: 24.2g - Carbs: 1.7g - Protein: 117.9g

Ingredients:

- 1 (12-pound) trimmed beef brisket
- ½ cup Worcestershire sauce
- 1 cup beef rub

Directions:

1. Coat brisket with Worcestershire sauce and sprinkle with rub evenly.
2. With a plastic wrap, cover the brisket and refrigerate for about 4 hours.
3. Remove brisket from refrigerator and keep aside, uncovered at room temperature for about 1 hour.
4. Preheat the pallet grill to 250-260 degrees F.
5. For coating mixture: in a bowl, add all ingredients and beat till well combined.
6. Arrange the brisket in pallet grill, fat-side down and cook, covered for about 5 hours.
7. Remove brisket from the pallet grill and wrap with a piece of foil tightly.
8. Arrange the brisket in pallet grill and cook for about 3-5 hours.
9. Remove the brisket from pallet grill and transfer onto a cutting board for about 10-15 minutes before slicing.
10. With a sharp knife, cut the brisket in desired sized slices and serve.

Astonishing Flank Steak (6 servings, serving: 1 portion)

Per Serving, Calories: 370 - Fat: 19.1g - Carbs: 0.1g - Protein: 46.8g

Ingredients:

- 1 (2-pound) beef flank steak
- 2 tablespoons olive oil
- ¼ cup BBQ rub
- 3 tablespoons crumbled blue cheese
- 2 tablespoons softened butter
- 1 teaspoon minced chives

Directions:

1. Preheat the pallet grill to 225 degrees F.
2. In a bowl, add blue cheese, butter and chives and mix well.
3. Coat the steak with oil evenly and season with BBQ rub.
4. Arrange the steak in pallet grill and cook for about 10-15 minutes per side.
5. Remove the steak from the pallet grill and transfer onto a cutting board for about 10 minutes before slicing.
6. With a sharp knife, cut the steak across the grain into thin strips.
7. Top with cheese mixture and serve.

Foolproof Strip Steak (2 servings, serving: 1 portion)

Per Serving, Calories: 220- Fat: 13.7g - Carbs: 0g - Protein: 23g

Ingredients:

- 2 (1-inch thick) strip steaks
- 2 teaspoons olive oil
- Kosher salt and freshly ground black pepper, to taste

Directions:

1. Preheat the pallet grill to 225 degrees F.
2. Coat the steaks with 1 teaspoon of oil and season with salt and black pepper evenly.
3. Arrange the steaks in pallet grill and cook for about 45-55 minutes.
4. Remove the steaks from the pallet grill and keep them warm.
5. Now, set the pallet grill to 700 F.
6. Now, arrange the steaks onto lower position of pallet grill and sear for about 3 minutes per side.
7. Serve immediately.

Elegant Steak (2 servings, serving: 1 portion)

Per Serving, Calories: 240- Fat: 16g - Carbs: 0g - Protein: 23g

Ingredients:

- 2 (1 3/8-inch thick) trimmed bone-in ribeye steaks
- 1 tablespoon olive oil
- 1 tablespoon steak seasoning

Directions:

1. Coat both sides of each steak with oil and season with steak seasoning.
2. Keep aside at room temperature for about 15 minutes.
3. Preheat the pallet grill to 325 degrees F.
4. Arrange the steaks in pallet grill and cook for about 15-20 minutes, flipping after every 6 minutes.
5. Serve immediately.

American Style Short Ribs (6 servings, serving: 1 portion)

Per Serving, Calories: 519- Fat: 22.2g - Carbs: 7.7g - Protein: 68g

Ingredients:

For Mustard Sauce:

- 1 cup prepared yellow mustard
- ¼ cup red wine vinegar
- ¼ cup dill pickle juice
- 2 tablespoons soy sauce
- 2 tablespoons Worcestershire sauce
- 1 teaspoon ground ginger
- 1 teaspoon granulated garlic

For Spice Rub:

- 2 tablespoons salt
- 2 tablespoons freshly ground black pepper
- 1 tablespoon white cane sugar
- 1 tablespoon granulated garlic

For Ribs:

- 6 (4-5-inch long) beef short ribs

Directions:

1. Preheat the pellet grill to 230-250 degrees F.
2. In a bowl, mix together all sauce ingredients.
3. In another bowl, mix together all rub ingredients.

4. Coat the ribs with sauce generously and sprinkle with spice rub evenly.

5. Arrange the ribs over greased grate, bone side down over indirect heat and cook, covered for bout 1-1½ hours.

6. Flip the side and cook for about 45 minutes.

7. Flip the side and cook for about 45 minutes more.

8. Remove the ribs from pallet grill and transfer onto a cutting board for about 10-15 minutes before slicing.

9. With a sharp knife, cut the ribs into equal sized individual ribs and serve.

Braised Short Ribs (6 servings, serving: 1 portion)

Per Serving, Calories: 573- Fat: 30.5g - Carbs: 7.3g - Protein: 55.5g

Ingredients:

- 2½ pound trimmed beef short ribs
- 4 tablespoons extra virgin olive oil
- 4 tablespoons beef rub
- 1 cup apple juice
- 1 cup apple cider vinegar
- 1 cup red wine
- 1 cup beef broth
- 2 tablespoons butter
- 2 tablespoons Worcestershire sauce
- Salt and freshly ground black pepper, to taste

Directions:

Preheat the pallet grill to 225 degrees F. Coat the ribs with olive oil and season with rub evenly. Arrange the ribs in pallet grill and cook for about 1 hour.

In a food-safe spray bottle, mix together apple juice and vinegar. Spray the ribs with vinegar mixture evenly. Cook for about 2 hours, spraying with vinegar mixture after every 15 minutes.

In a bowl, mix together remaining ingredients. Transfer the ribs in a baking dish with wine mixture. With a piece of foil, cover the baking dish tightly and cook for about 2-2½ hours.

Remove the ribs from pallet grill and transfer onto a cutting board for about 10-15 minutes before slicing. With a sharp knife, cut the ribs into equal sized individual ribs and serve.

Loveable Ribs (4 servings, serving: 1 portion)

Per Serving, Calories: 877 Fat: 51.7g - Carbs: 56.6g - Protein: 45.7g

Ingredients:

- 3 tablespoons kosher salt
- 3 tablespoons coarsely ground black pepper
- 2 racks beef back ribs

Directions:

1. Preheat the pallet grill to 225 degrees F.
2. In a small bowl, mix together salt and black pepper.
3. Season ribs with the salt mixture generously.
4. Arrange the rib rack in pallet grill and cook for about 5-6 hours.
5. Remove the rib rack from pallet grill and transfer onto a cutting board for about 10-15 minutes before slicing.
6. With a sharp knife, cut the ribs into equal sized individual ribs and serve.

Greatly Flavored Ribs (4 servings, serving: 1 portion)

Per Serving, Calories: 990- Fat: 59.8g - Carbs: 62.1g - Protein: 47.1g

Ingredients:

- 2 tablespoons butter
- 1 cup white vinegar
- 1 cup yellow mustard
- 2 tablespoons brown sugar
- 2 tablespoons Tabasco
- 1 teaspoon Worcestershire sauce
- 2 racks beef back ribs
- Kosher salt and freshly ground black pepper, to taste

Directions:

1. For BBQ sauce: in a pan, melt butter on medium heat. Stir in vinegar, mustard, brown sugar, Tabasco and Worcestershire sauce and remove from heat.

2. Keep aside to cool completely. Preheat the pallet grill to 225 degrees F.

3. Season the rib racks with salt and black pepper evenly. Coat rib rack with cooled sauce evenly. Arrange the rib racks in pallet grill and cook for about 5-6 hours, coating with sauce after every 2 hours.

4. Remove the rib racks from pallet grill and transfer onto a cutting board for about 10-15 minutes before slicing.

5. With a sharp knife, cut the rib racks into equal sized individual ribs and serve.

Healthy Beef Jerky (2-3 servings, serving: 1 portion)

Per Serving, Calories: 399- Fat:9.5g - Carbs: 25.3g - Protein: 48.9g

Ingredients:

- 4 minced garlic cloves
- ½ cup soy sauce
- ½ cup Worcestershire sauce
- ¼ cup brown sugar
- 2 teaspoons ground dried red chili
- 1 teaspoon onion powder
- Freshly ground black pepper, to taste
- 1 pound trimmed and cut into long thin strips top round steak

Detections:

1. In a bowl, add all ingredients except beef and mix till sugar is dissolved.
2. In a resealable plastic bag, add steak and marinade.
3. Seal the bag and shake to cot well.
4. Refrigerate for about 1-3 hours.
5. Preheat the pallet grill to 150 degrees F.
6. Arrange the beef strips in pallet grill and cook for about 3 hours.
7. Cover the strips with foil loosely and cook for about 1-2 hours.

Easy Pork Chops (4 servings, serving: 1 portion)

Per Serving, Calories: 316- Fat: 26.9g - Carbs: 0g - Protein: 18g

Ingredients:

- 4 (2-inch) thick cut pork chops
- 2 tablespoons olive oil
- Salt and freshly ground black pepper, to taste

Directions:

1. Preheat the pallet grill to 250 degrees F.
2. Coat pork chops with olive oil evenly and season with salt and black pepper generously.
3. Heat a nonstick skillet on high heat and sear the pork chops for about 1-2 minutes per side.
4. Now, arrange the seared pork chops in the pallet grill and cook, covered for about 1½ hours.
5. Remove the chops from the pallet grill and keep aside for about 5 minutes before serving.

Glorious Pork Chops (4 servings, serving: 1 portion)

Per Serving, Calories: 290- Fat: 20.2g - Carbs: 8.1g - Protein: 18.7g

Ingredients:

- 2 tablespoons crushed dried thyme
- 2 tablespoons dark brown sugar
- 1 tablespoon cayenne pepper
- 1 tablespoon onion powder
- 1 tablespoon garlic powder
- 4 bone-in, center cut pork chops

Directions:

1. In a bowl, mix together all ingredients except pork chops.
2. Rub the pork chops with spice mixture generously.
3. With a plastic wrap, cover the pork chops and refrigerate overnight.
4. Soak apple wood chips in water for at least 1 hour.
5. Preheat the pellet grill to 275 degrees F.
6. Place the chops in pallet grill and cook, covered for about 70 minutes.
7. Remove the chops from the pallet grill and keep aside for about 5 minutes before serving.

Premium Pork Chops (4 servings, serving: 1 portion)

Per Serving, Calories: 625- Fat: 20.5g - Carbs: 91.6g - Protein: 18.4g

Ingredients:

For Brine:

- 8 cups apple juice
- 1 cup light brown sugar
- ½ cup kosher salt
- ½ cup BBQ rub

For Pork Chops:

- 4 thick cut pork loin chops
- 2 tablespoons BBQ rub
- 1 tablespoon Montreal steak seasoning

Directions:

1. For brine: in a large pan, add 4 cups of apple juice and cook till heated completely. Add sugar, salt and dry rub and cook till dissolved, stirring continuously.

2. Remove from heat and stir in remaining apple juice. Keep aside to cool completely. In a larger ziplock, add brine mixture and chops.

3. Seal the bag and refrigerator for about 2 hours. Preheat the pellet grill to 250 degrees F. Remove the chops from brine and keep aside for about 10-15 minutes.

4. Now, season the chops with BBQ rub and steak seasoning evenly. Place the chops in pallet grill and cook, covered for about 1½ hours.

5. Remove the chops from the pallet grill and keep aside for about 5 minutes before serving.

Richly Spicy Pork Ribs (20 servings, serving: 1 portion)

Per Serving, Calories: 680- Fat: 54.4g - Carbs: 9.2g - Protein: 36.5g

Ingredients:

For Pork Rub:

- ¼ cup salt
- ¼ cup white sugar
- 2 tablespoons packed brown sugar
- 2 tablespoons ground white pepper
- 2 tablespoons ground black pepper
- 1 tablespoon red chili powder
- 1 tablespoon ground paprika
- 1 tablespoon ground cumin
- 1 tablespoon garlic powder
- 1 tablespoon onion powder
- 10 pound baby back pork ribs

For Sauce:

- 1 cup apple juice
- ¼ cup BBQ sauce
- ¼ cup packed brown sugar

Directions:

1. For spice mixture: in a bowl, mix together all ingredients.

2. Rub the ribs with spice mixture generously.

3. With a plastic wrap, cover the ribs and refrigerate for at least 30 minutes.

4. Preheat the pellet grill to 270 degrees F.

5. Arrange the ribs in the pallet grill and cook for about 1 hour.

6. Meanwhile, in a bowl, add apple juice, BBQ sauce and brown sugar and mix till well combined.

7. Coat the ribs with sauce and cook for about 3-4 hours, coating with sauce after every 3045 minutes.

8. Remove the rib racks from the pallet grill and keep aside for about 15 minutes before serving.

Tender Pork Ribs (16 servings, serving: 1 portion)

Per Serving, Calories: 658- Fat: 40.7g - Carbs: 7.7g - Protein: 61.1g

Ingredients:

- ¼ cup yellow honey mustard
- ¼ cup brown sugar
- 1/3 cup paprika
- ¼ cup garlic powder
- ¼ cup onion powder
- 2 tablespoons chipotle chili pepper flakes
- 2 tablespoons dried parsley flakes
- 1 tablespoon ground cumin
- Salt and freshly ground black pepper, to taste
- 8 pound silver skin removed pork loin baby back ribs

Directions:

1. In a bowl, add all ingredients except ribs and mx well. Rub the pork ribs with spice mixture generously.

2. Preheat the pellet grill to 200 degrees F.

3. Arrange the ribs in the pallet grill and cook for about 2 hours
Remove the ribs from the pallet grill and wrap in heavy duty foil.

4. Cook for about 2 hours more. Remove the foil and cook for about 1 hour more.

5. Remove the ribs from pallet grill and transfer onto a cutting board for about 10-15 minutes before serving.

Mouth Watering Pork Ribs (6 servings, serving: 1 portion)

Per Serving, Calories: 869- Fat: 52.8g - Carbs: 77.5g - Protein: 39.6g

Ingredients:

- 2 racks silver skin removed bone-in pork ribs
- 6-ounce BBQ rub
- 8-ounce apple juice
- ½ cup BBQ sauce

Directions:

1. Coat the rib racks with BBQ rub generously and keep aside for about 30 minutes.

2. Preheat the pellet grill to 225 degrees F. Arrange the ribs in the pallet grill, bone side down and cook for about 1 hour.

3. In a food-safe spray bottle, place apple juice. Spray the rib racks with vinegar mixture evenly. Cook for about 3½ hours, spraying with vinegar mixture after every 45 minutes.

4. Now, coat the rib racks with a light layer of BBQ sauce evenly and cook for about 10 minutes. After the sauce has set, take ribs off the grill and let rest for 10 minutes.

5. Remove the rib racks from pallet grill and transfer onto a cutting board for about 10-15 minutes before slicing.

6. With a sharp knife, cut the rib racks into equal sized individual ribs and serve.

Amazing Pork Butt Roast (16 servings, serving: 1 portion)

Per Serving, Calories: 398- Fat: 13.4.8g - Carbs: 2.2g - Protein: 61.9g

Ingredients:

For Injection:

- 1 cup apple juice
- 1 cup apple cider vinegar

For Pork Rub:

- 1 (7-pound) trimmed pork butt
- 3 tablespoons Dijon mustard
- ¼ cup spice rub

For Spritz:

- 1 cup apple cider vinegar
- 1 cup water

Directions:

For injection: in a bowl, mix together apple juice and vinegar. With a baster-injector, inject pork butt with apple juice mixture Rub pork but with mustard and spice rub evenly.

Arrange pork but in a baking dish and refrigerate for at least 1 hour. Preheat the pellet grill to 250 degrees F. Arrange the pork butt in pallet grill, fat side up and cook for about 3 hours.

In a food-safe spray bottle, mix together vinegar and water. Spray the pork roast with vinegar mixture evenly. Cook for about 2 hours, spraying with vinegar mixture after every 15 minutes. Now, place the pork into a roasting pan with about 2 tablespoons of spritz.

With a piece of foil, cover the pan tightly and cook till the internal temperature of meat reaches between 200-203 degrees F. Remove the roast from pallet grill and transfer onto a cutting board for about 10-15 minutes before slicing. With a sharp knife, cut the roast in desired sized slices and serve.

Nicely Flavored Pork Butt Roast (14 servings, serving: 1 portion)

Per Serving, Calories: 452- Fat: 15.1g - Carbs: 3.4g - Protein: 70.8g

Ingredients:

- ¼ cup brown sugar
- 2 tablespoons New Mexico chile powder
- 2 tablespoons garlic powder
- Salt, to taste
- 1 (7-pound) fresh pork butt roast

Directions:

1. Preheat the pellet grill to 200-225 degrees F.
2. In a bowl, mix together all ingredients except pork roast.
3. Rub the pork roast with spice mixture generously.
4. Arrange a roasting rack in a drip pan.
5. Place the pork roast over rack and cook for about 6-14 hours or till desired doneness.
6. Remove the roast from pallet grill and transfer onto a cutting board for about 10-15 minutes before slicing.
7. With a sharp knife, cut the roast in desired sized slices and serve.

Authentic Butt Roast (6 servings, serving: 1 portion)

Per Serving, Calories: 703- Fat: 36.5g - Carbs: 8.4g - Protein: 84.2g

Ingredients:

For Pork:

- 1 tablespoon crushed dried oregano
- 3 tablespoons smoked paprika
- 2 tablespoons chili powder
- 2 tablespoons cayenne pepper
- 2 tablespoons ground cumin
- Salt and freshly ground black pepper, to taste
- 1 (3½-pound) Boston butt
- 3 tablespoons yellow mustard

For Coating:

- ½ cup olive oil
- ½ cup apple juice

Directions:

For spice mixture: in a bowl, mix together oregano and all spices. Coat the pork butt with mustard in a thin layer. Season the pork butt with spice mixture generously.

With a plastic wrap, cover the pork butt and refrigerate for at least 8 hours. Preheat the pellet grill to 225 degrees F. Remove the pork butt from the refrigerator and keep aside at room temperature for at least 30 minutes before cooking.

Arrange the pork butt in the pallet grill, fat side up and cook for about 4-6 hours, coating with oil mixture after every 2 hours. Remove the roast from pallet grill and transfer onto a cutting board for about 10-15 minutes before slicing. With a sharp knife, cut the roast in desired sized slices and serve.

Tender Pork Shoulder (20 servings, serving: 1 portion)

Per Serving, Calories: 516- Fat: 37.1g - Carbs: 12.7g - Protein: 30.9g

Ingredients:

For Rub:

- 5 tablespoons light brown sugar
- 5 tablespoons white sugar
- 2 tablespoons paprika
- 1 tablespoon garlic powder
- 1 tablespoon onion powder
- 1 tablespoon freshly ground black pepper
- Salt, to taste

For Roast:

- 4 cups apple cider
- 1 (8-pound) pork shoulder roast
- 1 chopped onion

Directions:

In a bowl, mix together all rub ingredients. In a large bowl, mix together about ¼ cup of rub mixture and apple cider. Add pork shoulder and coat with mixture evenly. Refrigerate, covered for about 12 hours. Preheat the pallet grill to 210 degrees F.

Remove pork shoulder from bowl. In water pan of pallet grill, add cider marinade, onion and about ¼ cup of rub mixture. Rub the pork shoulder with remaining rub mixture evenly.

Arrange pork shoulder in the center of pallet grill and cook for about 8 hours. Remove the pork shoulder from pallet grill and transfer onto a cutting board for about 30 minutes before shredding. With 2 forks, shred the pork shoulder and serve.

Crowd Pleasing Pork Belly (13 servings, serving: 1 portion)

Per Serving, Calories: 805- Fat: 47g - Carbs: 0g - Protein: 80.5g

Ingredients:

- 1 (5-pound) skin removed pork belly
- Kosher salt and coarsely ground black pepper, to taste

Directions:

1. Preheat the pellet grill to 225 degrees F.
2. Rub the pork belly with salt and black pepper generously.
3. Arrange the pork belly in the pallet grill and cook for about 6-8 hours,
4. Remove the pork belly from pallet grill and transfer onto a cutting board for about 10-15 minutes before slicing.
5. With a sharp knife, cut the pork belly in desired sized slices and serve.

Delightfully Perfect Pork Belly (10 servings, serving: 1 portion)

Per Serving, Calories: 879- Fat: 49g - Carbs: 10.1g - Protein: 83.8g

Ingredients:

- 1 (4-pound) pork belly
- ¼ cup sweet rub
- 2 cups apple juice, divided
- ½ cup BBQ sauce

Directions:

1. Preheat the pallet grill to 225 degrees F.

2. With a sharp knife, score the top layer of fat on the pork belly in 1-inch squares. Season pork belly with sweet rub generously. In a food-safe spray bottle, add 1½ cups of apple juice.

3. Arrange the pork belly in the pallet grill and cook for about 6 hours, spraying with apple juice after every 1 hour.

4. Remove the belly from the grill. Wrap the pork belly in a heavy-duty tinfoil with remaining ½ cup of the apple juice.

5. Seal the edges of foil completely and cook for 1¼-1½ hours till the internal temperature reaches to 200 degrees F.

6. Carefully, remove the belly from foil and drizzle with the apple juices from foil. Coat the pork belly with BBQ sauce and cook for about 10 minutes.

7. Remove the pork belly from pallet grill and transfer onto a cutting board for about 10-15 minutes before slicing.

8. With a sharp knife, cut the pork belly in desired sized slices and serve.

Chinese Favorite Pork Belly (10 servings, serving: 1 portion)

Per Serving, Calories: 878- Fat: 49g - Carbs: 8.2g - Protein: 84.4g

Ingredients:

- ½ cup pineapple juice
- 3 tablespoons hoisin sauce
- 2 tablespoons soy sauce
- 2 tablespoons honey
- 1½ tablespoons dry sherry
- ½ teaspoon Chinese five spice powder
- 5 finely minced garlic cloves
- Kosher salt and freshly ground black pepper, to taste
- 1 (4-pound) skin-on pork belly

Directions:

In a bowl, add all ingredients except pork belly and mix till well combined. With a sharp knife, score the skin of the pork belly into ¼-inch diamond pattern.

In a large resealable plastic bag, add marinade and pork belly. Seal the bag and shake to coat evenly. Refrigerate for at least 4 hours to overnight. Remove pork belly from bag and keep aside at room temperature for about 30 minutes.

Preheat the pallet grill to 225 degrees F.

Arrange the pork belly in the pallet grill, skin side up and cook for about 4-5 hours. Meanwhile, preheat the broiler of oven. Remove pork belly from grill and place into a broiler pan, skin side up. Broil for about 4-5 minutes or till crisp.

Remove the pork belly from oven and transfer onto a cutting board for about 10-15 minutes before slicing. With a sharp knife, cut the pork belly in desired sized slices and serve.

Welcoming Pork Tenderloin (6 servings, serving: 1 portion)

Per Serving, Calories: 498- Fat: 18.4g - Carbs: 11.1g - Protein: 67.8g

Ingredients:

- ½ cup apple cider
- 3 tablespoons honey
- 2 (1¼-1½-pound) silver skin removed pork tenderloins
- 3 tablespoons sweet rub

Directions:

1. In a small bowl, mix together apple cider and honey.
2. Coat the outside of tenderloins with honey mixture and season with the rub generously.
3. With plastic wraps, cover the tenderloins and refrigerate for about 2-3 hours.
4. Preheat the pallet grill to 225 degrees F.
5. Arrange the tenderloins in the pallet grill and cook for about 2½-3 hours.
6. Remove the pork tenderloins from the pallet grill and transfer onto a cutting board for about 5 minutes before slicing.
7. With a sharp knife, cut the pork tenderloins in desired sized slices and serve.

Party Dinner Pork Loin (10 servings, serving: 1 portion)

Per Serving, Calories: 571- Fat: 29.6g - Carbs: 24.7g - Protein: 49.9g

Ingredients:

- 1 (4-pound) silver skin removed pork loin
- 3 tablespoons olive oil
- 3 tablespoons spice rub
- 1 (10-ounce) jar seedless raspberry jam
- 1 (5-ounce) bottle Tabasco sauce

Directions:

Preheat the pallet grill to 230 degrees F.

Season the loin with the rub generously. Arrange the tenderloins in the pallet grill and cook for about 1½-2 hours.

Remove pork from pallet grill and wrap in a piece of foil lightly.

Meanwhile, preheat the broiler of oven. In a bowl, add jam and Tabasco sauce and mix well.

Unwrap the pork and coat with the glaze evenly. Arrange pork loin onto a broiler pan and broil for about 3 minutes.

Remove the pork loin from the pallet grill and transfer onto a cutting board for about 5 minutes before slicing.

With a sharp knife, cut the pork loin in desired sized slices and serve.

Holiday Special Ham (14 servings, serving: 1 portion)

Per Serving, Calories: 391- Fat: 19.1g - Carbs: 21.4g - Protein: 32.9g

Ingredients:

For Ham:

- 1 tablespoon sugar
- 1 tablespoon paprika
- 1 tablespoon freshly ground black pepper
- 1 teaspoon mustard powder
- ½ teaspoon cayenne pepper
- Salt, to taste
- 1 (6-pound) ready-to-eat ham

For Sauce:

- ¾ cup chicken broth
- ¾ cup pineapple juice
- 2 tablespoons olive oil
- ½ teaspoon ground cloves
- ½ teaspoon mustard powder

For Glaze:

- ½ cup honey
- ¼ cup pineapple juice
- ½ teaspoon mustard powder
- Pinch of ground cloves

Directions:

1. For ham: in a bowl, add all ingredients except ham and mix well.
2. Rub the ham with mixture generously.
3. With a piece of foil, cover the ham and refrigerate overnight.
4. Remove ham from refrigerator and keep at room temperature for about 1 hour.
5. Meanwhile for sauce in a pan, mix together all ingredients on medium heat.
6. Cook till the sauce becomes warm enough, stirring continuously.
7. Preheat the pallet grill to 210 degrees F.
8. Arrange the ham in pallet grill and cook for about 6 hours, coating with sauce after every 1 hour.
9. For glaze: in a bowl, mix together all ingredients.
10. During last1 hour of cooking, coat the ham with glaze twice generously.
11. Remove the ham from pallet grill and transfer onto a cutting board for about 20-25 minutes before serving.
12. With a sharp knife, cut the ham in desired sized slices and serve.

Sweetly Delicious Ham (18 servings, serving: 1 portion)

Per Serving, Calories: 482- Fat: 21.7g - Carbs: 28.2g - Protein: 41.9g

Ingredients:

For Sauce:

- ½ cup apple juice
- ½ cup orange juice
- ¼ cup honey
- ¼ cup brown sugar
- 2 tablespoons maple syrup

For Rub:

- ½ cup dark brown sugar
- ¼ cup white sugar
- ¼ cup turbinado sugar
- ½ teaspoon paprika
- ½ teaspoon ground cinnamon
- ½ teaspoon ground ginger
- ½ teaspoon ground nutmeg

For Ham:

- 1 (10-pound) spiral sliced Ham (shank portion)

Directions:

1. Preheat the pallet grill to 225-250 degrees F.
2. For sauce: in a bowl, add all ingredients and mix till well combined.
3. For rub: in a bowl, mix together all ingredients.
4. Arrange ham over a piece of foil, meat side down.
5. Coat ham with sauce evenly and then, season with rub mixture evenly.
6. Arrange the ham in pallet grill and cook for about 2½ hours, coating with sauce occasionally.
7. Remove the ham from pallet grill and transfer onto a cutting board for about 20-25 minutes before serving.
8. With a sharp knife, cut the ham in desired sized slices and serve.

Christmas Table Ham (18 servings, serving: 1 portion)

Per Serving, Calories: 603- Fat: 21.9g - Carbs: 52.3g - Protein: 42g

Ingredients:

- 18-ounce pineapple preserves
- 1 cup Bourbon
- 1 cup honey
- ½ cup brown sugar
- 1/3 cup dark molasses
- 1/3 cup spice rub
- 1 tablespoon ground mustard
- 1 (10-pound) spiral sliced Ham

Directions:

1. In a pan, add all ingredients except ham on low heat and cook for about 20 minutes, stirring occasionally.
2. Remove from heat and keep aside to cool completely.
3. Preheat the pallet grill to 225 degrees F.
4. Arrange the ham in pallet grill and cook for about 6 hours
5. During last1 hour of cooking, coat the ham with glaze after every 15 minutes.
6. Remove the ham from pallet grill and transfer onto a cutting board for about 20-25 minutes before serving.
7. With a sharp knife, cut the ham in desired sized slices and serve.

Classic Ham (12 servings, serving: 1 portion)

Per Serving, Calories: 610 Fat: 30.9g - Carbs: 39.6g - Protein: 44.2g

Ingredients:

- 1 cup honey
- ¼ cup dark corn syrup
- 1 (7-pound) ready-to-eat ham
- ¼ cup whole cloves
- ½ cup softened butter

Directions:

1. Preheat the pallet grill to 325 degrees F.
2. In a small pan, add honey and corn syrup and cook till heated slightly, stirring continuously.
3. Remove from heat. With a sharp knife, score the ham in a cross pattern.
4. Insert whole cloves at the crossings. Coat the ham with butter evenly.
5. Arrange ham in foil lined roasting pan and top with ¾ of glaze evenly.
6. Arrange the pan in pallet grill and cook for about 1¼ hours, coating with remain glaze after every 10-15 minutes.
7. Remove the ham from pallet grill and transfer onto a cutting board for about 20-25 minutes before serving.
8. With a sharp knife, cut the ham in desired sized slices and serve.

Holiday Feast Ham (24-26 servings, serving: 1 portion)

Per Serving, Calories: 507 Fat: 23g - Carbs: 29.1g - Protein: 44.1g

Ingredients:

- 1 (12-15-pound) cured ham
- 12-ounce Dijon mustard
- 1 pound brown sugar, divided
- 1 cup pineapple juice

Directions:

1. Preheat the pellet grill to 325 degrees F.

2. Coat ham with Dijon mustard evenly and then sprinkle with brown sugar slightly. Arrange ham in the pellet grill and cook for about 2 hours.

3. Remove the ham from pellet grill and place over a piece of foil. Coat the ham with pineapple juice evenly.

4. Now, set the pallet grill to 225 degrees F. Wrap the ham in foil and cook in the pellet grill for about 1 hour.

5. Unwrap the top of ham and sprinkle with brown sugar generously. Coat with glaze and baste with pineapple juice. Cook in the pellet grill for about 1 hour.

6. Remove the ham from pallet grill and transfer onto a cutting board for about 20-25 minutes before serving.

7. With a sharp knife, cut the ham in desired sized slices and serve.

Breakfast Sausage (6 servings, serving: 1 portion)

Per Serving, Calories: 513 Fat: 42.9g - Carbs: 0g - Protein: 29.4g

Ingredients:

- 2 pound fresh Italian sausage in casings

Directions:

1. Preheat the pallet grill to 250 degrees F.

2. Arrange the sausage links in pallet grill about /2-inch apart and cook for about 3 hours.

Zesty Sausage (6 servings, serving: 1 portion)

Per Serving, Calories: 399 Fat: 27.9g - Carbs: 17.3g - Protein: 19.3g

Ingredients:

- ½ cup apricot jam
- 1 tablespoon Dijon mustard
- 12 breakfast sausage links

Directions:

1. In a small pan, add jam and mustard on medium-low heat and cook till warmed. Place on low heat to keep warm. Preheat the pallet grill to 350 degrees F.

2. Arrange the sausage links in pallet grill and cook for about 10-15 minutes, flipping twice.

3. Coat sausages with jam glaze evenly and cook for about 2-3 minutes. Serve alongside remaining glaze.

Delightful Sausage (5 servings, serving: 1 portion)

Per Serving, Calories: 467 Fat: 27.8g - Carbs: 13.8g - Protein: 20.8g

Ingredients:

- 4 (12-ounce) cans beer
- 2 sliced into rings large onions
- 10 uncooked brats

Directions:

Preheat the pallet grill to 350 degrees F. In a large pan, add beer and onions and bring to a gentle boil.

Arrange a deep disposable aluminum foil pan on one side of the pallet grill. Carefully, transfer the beer mixture into the foil pan on the grill.

Arrange the brats on the other side of the grill grate and cook for about 20-25 minutes, flipping frequently.

Transfer the brats into the beer mixture and with a piece of foil, cover the pan tightly.

Cook for about 45-60 minutes.

Enticing Lamb Chops (6 servings, serving: 1 portion)

Per Serving, Calories: 376- Fat: 19.5g - Carbs: 0g - Protein: 47.8g

Ingredients:

- 6 (6-ounce) lamb chops
- 3 tablespoons olive oil
- Salt and freshly ground black pepper, to taste

Directions:

1. Preheat the pallet grill to 450 degrees F.
2. Coat the lamb chops with oil and then, season with salt and black pepper evenly.
3. Arrange the chops in pallet grill grate and cook for about 4-6 minutes per side.

Favorite Lamb Shoulder Chops (4 servings, serving: 1 portion)

Per Serving, Calories: 328- Fat: 18.2g - Carbs: 11.7g - Protein: 30.1g

Ingredients:

- 4 lamb shoulder chops
- 4 cups buttermilk
- 1 cup cold water
- ¼ cup kosher salt
- 2 tablespoons olive oil
- 1 tablespoon Texas style rub

Directions:

In a large bowl, add buttermilk, water and salt and stir till salt is dissolved.

Add chops and coat with mixture evenly.

Refrigerate for at least 4 hours. Remove the chops from bowl and rinse under cold water.

Coat the chops with olive oil and then sprinkle with rub evenly. Preheat the pallet grill to 240 degrees F.

Arrange the chops in pallet grill grate and cook for about 25-30 minute or till desired doneness.

Meanwhile preheat the broiler of oven.

Cook the chops under broiler till browned.

Irresistible Lamb Ribs Rack (2 servings, serving: 1 portion)

Per Serving, Calories: 1087- Fat: 70g - Carbs: 13.7g - Protein: 96.6g

Ingredients:

- 2 tablespoons fresh sage
- 2 tablespoons fresh rosemary
- 2 tablespoons fresh thyme
- 2 peeled garlic cloves
- 1 tablespoon honey
- Salt and freshly ground black pepper, to taste
- ¼ cup olive oil
- 1 (1½-pound) trimmed rack lamb ribs

Directions:

1. In a food processor, add all ingredients except oil and lamb rack and pulse till well combined.

2. While motor is running, slowly add oil and pulse till a smooth paste is formed.

3. Coat the rib rack with paste generously and refrigerate for about 2 hours.

4. Preheat the pallet grill to 225 degrees F.

5. Arrange the rib rack in pallet grill and cook for about 2 hours.
Remove the rib rack from pallet grill and transfer onto a cutting board for about 10-15 minutes before slicing.

6. With a sharp knife, cut the rib rack into equal sized individual ribs and serve.

Delicious Lamb Ribs Rack (8 servings, serving: 1 portion)

Per Serving, Calories: 826- Fat: 44.1g - Carbs: 5.4g - Protein: 96.3g

Ingredients:

- 4 (1-1½-pound) trimmed rack lamb ribs
- 1 tablespoon unsweetened cocoa powder
- 1 tablespoon brown sugar
- 1 tablespoon smoked paprika
- 1 tablespoon salt
- 1 tablespoon cracked black pepper
- 1 cup cherry cola

Directions:

1. Preheat the pallet grill to 225 degrees F.
2. With a sharp knife, make ½x¼-inchcuts in each rib rack.
3. In a bowl, mix together remaining ingredients except cherry cola.
4. Rub the rib racks with sugar mixture generously.
5. Arrange the rib racks in pallet grill and cook for about 2½-3 hours, coating with cherry cola after every 1 hour.
6. Remove the rib racks from pallet grill and transfer onto a cutting board for about 10-15 minutes before slicing.
7. With a sharp knife, cut the rib racks into equal sized individual ribs and serve.

Spice Crusted Ribs Rack (4 servings, serving: 1 portion)

Per Serving, Calories: 818- Fat: 44.5g - Carbs: 2.6g - Protein: 96.6g

Ingredients:

- 2 tablespoons paprika
- ½ tablespoon coriander seeds
- 1 teaspoon cumin seeds
- 1 teaspoon ground allspice
- 1 teaspoon powdered lemon peel
- Salt and freshly ground black pepper, to taste
- 2 (1½-pound) trimmed rack lamb ribs

Directions:

1. Preheat the pallet grill to 225 degrees F.
2. In a coffee grinder, add all ingredients except rib racks and grind into a powder.
3. Coat the rib racks with spice mixture generously.
4. Arrange the rib racks in pallet grill and cook for about 3 hours.
5. Remove the rib racks from pallet grill and transfer onto a cutting board for about 10-15 minutes before slicing.
6. With a sharp knife, cut the rib racks into equal sized individual ribs and serve.

Effortless Lamb Ribs Rack (3 servings, serving: 1 portion)

Per Serving, Calories: 1441- Fat: 78.5g - Carbs: 2.1g - Protein: 170.7g

Ingredients:

- 3 tablespoons minced fresh rosemary
- Salt and freshly ground black pepper, to taste
- 1 (4-pound) trimmed rack lamb ribs

Directions:

1. Preheat the pallet grill to 225 degrees F.
2. In a bowl, mix together rosemary, salt and black pepper.
3. Rub ribs rack with rosemary mixture generously.
4. Arrange the rib rack in pallet grill and cook, covered for about 1½-2 hours.
5. Remove the rib rack from pallet grill and transfer onto a cutting board for about 10-15 minutes before slicing.
6. With a sharp knife, cut the rib rack into equal sized individual ribs and serve.

Distinctive Lamb Shank (6 servings, serving: 1 portion)

Per Serving, Calories: 1115- Fat: 41.7g - Carbs: 2.2g - Protein: 159.4g

Ingredients:

- 8-ounce red wine
- 2-ounce whiskey
- 2 tablespoons minced fresh rosemary
- 1 tablespoon minced garlic
- Salt and freshly ground black pepper, to taste
- 6 (1¼-pound) lamb shanks

Directions:

1. In a bowl, add all ingredients except lamb shank and mix till well combined.
2. In a large resealable bag, add marinade and lamb shank.
3. Seal the bag and shake to coat completely.
4. Refrigerate for about 24 hours.
5. Preheat the pallet grill to 225 degrees F.
6. Arrange the leg of lamb in pallet grill and cook for about 4 hours.

Succulent Lamb Shank (2 servings, serving: 1 portion)

Per Serving, Calories: 1507- Fat: 62g - Carbs: 68.7g - Protein: 163.3g

Ingredients:

- 2 (1¼-pound) lamb shanks
- 1-2 cups water
- ½ cup brown sugar
- ½ cup rice wine
- ½ cup soy sauce
- 3 tablespoons dark sesame oil
- 4 (1½x½-inch) orange zest strips
- 2 (3-inch long) cinnamon sticks
- 1½ teaspoon Chinese five spice powder

Directions:

1. Preheat the pallet grill to 225-250 degrees F.
2. With a sharp knife, pierce each lamb shank at many places.
3. In a bowl, add remaining all ingredients and mix till sugar is dissolved.
4. In a large roasting pan, place lamb shanks and top with sugar mixture evenly.
5. Place the foil pan in pallet grill and cook for about 8-10 hours, flipping after every 30 minutes. (If required, add enough water to keep the liquid ½-inch over).

Scrumptious Lamb Shank (4 servings, serving: 1 portion)

Per Serving, Calories: 1155- Fat: 34.4g - Carbs: 15.2g - Protein: 159.7g

Ingredients:

- 4 (1¼-pound) lamb shanks
- 2 tablespoons Dijon mustard
- 4 teaspoons Italian seasoning
- Salt and freshly ground black pepper, to taste
- ½ cup red wine
- Water, as required
- 2 fresh rosemary sprigs
- 2 cups apple juice

Directions:

1. Preheat the pallet grill to 225-250 degrees F.
2. Coat the shanks with mustard and then, sprinkle with Italian seasoning, salt and black pepper.
3. In the diffuser pan, add red wine, rosemary sprigs and enough water to fill.
4. In a food-safe spray bottle, mix together apple juice and vinegar.
5. Arrange the shank in pallet grill and cook for about 5 hours, spraying with apple juice after every 30 minutes.

Festive Leg of Lamb (10 servings, serving: 1 portion)

Per Serving, Calories: 715- Fat: 38.9g - Carbs: 2.2g - Protein: 84.6g

Ingredients:

For Filling:

- 1 (8-ounce) package softened cream cheese
- ¼ cup cooked and crumbled bacon
- 1 seeded and chopped jalapeño pepper

For Spice Mixture:

- 1 tablespoon crushed dried rosemary
- 2 teaspoons garlic powder
- 1 teaspoon onion powder
- 1 teaspoon paprika
- 1 teaspoon cayenne pepper
- Salt, to taste

For Leg of Lamb:

- 1 (4-5-pound) butterflied leg of lamb
- 2-3 tablespoons olive oil

Directions:

1. For filling in a bowl, add all ingredients and mix till well combined.

2. For spice mixture in another small bowl, mix together all ingredients.

3. Place the leg of lamb onto a smooth surface. Sprinkle the inside of leg with some spice mixture.

4. Place filling mixture over the inside surface evenly. Roll the leg of lamb tightly and with a butcher's twine, tie the roll to secure the filling

5. Coat the outer side of roll with olive oil evenly and then sprinkle with spice mixture.

6. Preheat the pallet grill to 225-240 degrees F.

7. Arrange the leg of lamb in pallet grill and cook for about 2-2½ hours. Remove the leg of lamb from pallet grill and transfer onto a cutting board.

8. With a piece of foil, cover leg loosely and transfer onto a cutting board for about 20-25 minutes before slicing.

9. With a sharp knife, cut the leg of lamb in desired sized slices and serve.

Restaurant Style Leg of Lamb (6 servings, serving: 1 portion)

Per Serving, Calories: 508- Fat: 25.6g - Carbs: 1.9g - Protein: 64.4g

Ingredients:

- ¼ cup fresh lemon juice
- ¼ cup extra-virgin olive oil
- ¼ cup Dijon mustard
- ½ tablespoon crushed dried oregano
- ½ tablespoon crushed dried rosemary
- 4 minced garlic cloves
- Salt and freshly ground black pepper, to taste
- 1 (3-pound) boneless leg of lamb

Directions:

In a bowl, add all ingredients except leg of lamb and mix till well combined.

In a large resealable bag, add marinade and leg of lamb. Seal the bag and shake to coat completely. Refrigerate overnight.

Preheat the pallet grill to 300 degrees F.

Place an aluminum pan filled with water in the center of the lower grate. Remove the leg of lamb from the marinade and with paper towels, pat dry it.

Arrange the leg of lamb on the main grilling grate directly above the aluminum pan and cook, covered for about 1 hour.

Remove the leg of lamb from the pallet grill and transfer onto a cutting board for about 20 minutes before slicing.

With a sharp knife, cut the leg of lamb in desired sized slices and serve.

Luxurious Leg of Lamb (8 servings, serving: 1 portion)

Per Serving, Calories: 650- Fat: 33.4g - Carbs: 2.1g - Protein: 79.7g

Ingredients:

- ½ cup olive oil
- ½ cup wine vinegar
- ½ cup dry white wine
- 1 tablespoon minced garlic
- 1 teaspoon crushed dried marjoram
- 1 teaspoon crushed dried rosemary
- Salt and freshly ground black pepper, to taste
- 1 (5-pound) leg of lamb

Directions:

1. In a bowl, add all ingredients except leg of lamb and mix till well combined.
2. In a large resealable bag, add marinade and leg of lamb.
3. Seal the bag and shake to coat completely. Refrigerate for about 4-6 hours, flipping occasionally.
4. Preheat the pallet grill to 225 degrees F.
5. Arrange the leg of lamb in pallet grill and cook, covered for about 4-5 hours.
6. Remove the leg of lamb from the pallet grill and transfer onto a cutting board for about 20 minutes before slicing.
7. With a sharp knife, cut the leg of lamb in desired sized slices and serve.

Appetizing Lamb Shoulder (8 servings, serving: 1 portion)

Per Serving, Calories: 585- Fat: 24.4g - Carbs: 4.3g - Protein: 79.7g

Ingredients:

- 1 tablespoon dried rosemary
- Salt and freshly ground black pepper, to taste
- 1 (5-pound) trimmed boneless lamb shoulder
- 2 cups apple cider vinegar, divided
- 2 tablespoons olive oil
- 1 cup apple juice

Directions:

1. Preheat the pallet grill to 225 degrees F.
2. In a bowl, mix together rosemary, salt and black pepper.
3. With a baster-injector, inject lamb shoulder with 1 cup of vinegar.
4. Coat lamb shoulder with oil and then season rosemary mixture evenly.
5. With kitchen twine, tie the lamb shoulder tightly Arrange lamb shoulder in pallet grill and cook for about 1 hour.
6. In a food-safe spray bottle, mix together remaining vinegar and apple juice.
7. Spray the lamb shoulder with vinegar mixture evenly. Cook for about 3 hours, spraying with vinegar mixture after every 15 minutes.
8. Now with a piece of foil, cover the lamb shoulder and cook till the internal temperature reaches to 195 degrees F.
9. Remove the lamb shoulder from the pallet grill and transfer onto a cutting board for about 20 minutes before slicing. With a sharp knife, cut the lamb shoulder in desired sized slices and serve.

Luscious Lamb Shoulder (8 servings, serving: 1 portion)

Per Serving, Calories: 569- Fat: 24.6g - Carbs: 2.2g - Protein: 80g

Ingredients:

- 1 (5-pound) trimmed bon-in lamb shoulder
- 2 tablespoons olive oil
- 1 tablespoon fresh lemon juice
- 1 tablespoon peeled fresh ginger
- 4-6 peeled garlic cloves
- ½ tablespoon ground cumin
- ½ tablespoon paprika
- ½ tablespoon ground turmeric
- ½ tablespoon ground allspice
- Salt and freshly ground black pepper, to taste

Directions:

With a sharp knife, score the skin of the lamb shoulder into diamond pattern. In a food processor, add remaining all ingredients and pule till smooth.

Coat the lamb shoulder with pureed mixture generously. Arrange the lamb shoulder into a large baking dish and refrigerate, covered overnight.

Remove from refrigerator and keep at room temperature for at least 1 hour before cooking.

Preheat the pallet grill to 225 degrees F. Arrange lamb shoulder in pallet grill and cook for about 2½ hours. Remove the lamb shoulder from the pallet grill and transfer onto a cutting board for about 20 minutes before slicing.

With a sharp knife, cut the lamb shoulder in desired sized slices and serve.

Simply Delicious Lamb Breast (2 servings, serving: 1 portion)

Per Serving, Calories: 877- Fat: 34.5g - Carbs: 2.2g - Protein: 128.7g

Ingredients:

- 1 (2-pound) trimmed bone-in lamb breast
- ½ cup white vinegar
- ¼ cup yellow mustard
- ½ cup BBQ rub

Directions:

1. Preheat the pallet grill to 225 degrees F.
2. Rinse the lamb breast with vinegar evenly.
3. Coat lamb breast with mustard and the, season with BBQ rub evenly.
4. Arrange lamb breast in pallet grill and cook for about 2-2½ hours.
5. Remove the lamb breast from the pallet grill and transfer onto a cutting board for about 10 minutes before slicing.
6. With a sharp knife, cut the lamb breast in desired sized slices and serve.

Best-Ever Flounder Parcel (2 servings, serving: 1 portion)

Per Serving, Calories: 120- Fat: 8g - Carbs: 1.9g - Protein: 10.9g

Ingredients:

- 1 scaled whole flounder
- 1 tablespoon olive oil
- 1 tablespoon fresh lemon juice
- 2 tablespoons finely chopped fresh dill
- Salt and freshly ground black pepper, to taste
- ½ of thinly sliced lemon

Directions:

1. Preheat the pallet grill to 350 degrees F.
2. With a sharp knife, make 3-4 diagonal slits in the flounder.
3. Drizzle the flounder with olive oil and lemon juice evenly.
4. Rub the flounder with dill, salt and black pepper.
5. Insert the lemon slices in slits firmly.
6. Arrange the flounder over a piece of foil.
7. Fold the sides up, high around the flounder.
8. Arrange the flounder parcel in pallet grill and cook, covered for about 10 minutes or till desired doneness.

Crispy Trout (6 servings, serving: 1 portion)

Per Serving, Calories: 287- Fat: 12.8g - Carbs: 0g - Protein: 40.3g

Ingredients:

- ½ cup salt
- 4 cups water
- 2 pound skin on, pin bones removed trout fillets

Directions:

1. For brine: in a large bowl, dissolve salt in water.
2. Add trout fillets and refrigerate, covered for about 3 hours.
3. Remove trout from brine and rinse under cold water.
4. With paper towels, pat dry the trout fillets.
5. Arrange a cooling rack in a sheet pan.
6. Place the trout fillets onto cooling rack, skin side down.
7. Refrigerate for about 22-24 hours.
8. Preheat the pallet grill to 150-160 degrees F, using charcoal.
9. Arrange the trout fillets in pallet grill and cook for about 2½-3 hours or till desired doneness.

Trout (8 servings, serving: 1 portion)

Per Serving, Calories: 577- Fat: 24g - Carbs: 9.7g - Protein: 75.9g

Ingredients:

- 8 cups water
- ½ cup brown sugar
- ¼ cup salt
- 1 tablespoon ground black pepper
- 2 tablespoons soy sauce
- 8 (10-ounce) butterflied rainbow trout

Directions:

1. For brine: in a large bucket, add all ingredients except trout and stir till sugar and salt are dissolved.
2. Add trout and keep aside for about 1 hour.
3. Preheat the pallet grill to 225 degrees F.
4. Remove trout from brine and with paper towels, pat dry completely.
5. Arrange the trout in pallet grill and cook for about ½-2 hours or till desired doneness.
6. Serve hot.

Lively flavored Trout (5 servings, serving: 1 portion)

Per Serving, Calories: 1078- Fat: 15.5g - Carbs: 3.9g - Protein: 159.1g

Ingredients:

- 1 (7-pound) butterflied whole lake trout
- ½ cup kosher salt
- ½ cup chopped fresh rosemary
- 2 teaspoons finely grated lemon zest

Directions:

1. Rub the trout with salt generously and then, sprinkle with rosemary and lemon zest.
2. Arrange the trout in a large baking dish and refrigerate for about 7-8 hours.
3. Remove from baking dish and rinse under cold running water.
4. With paper towels, pat dry the trout fillets.
5. Arrange a cooling rack in a sheet pan.
6. Place the trout fillets onto cooling rack, skin side down.
7. Refrigerate for about 24 hours.
8. Preheat the pallet grill to 180 degrees F, using charcoal.
9. Arrange the trout fillets in pallet grill and cook for about 2-4 hours or till desired doneness.
10. Serve hot.

Citrus Salmon (6 servings, serving: 1 portion)

Per Serving, Calories: 2051- Fat: 9.4g - Carbs: 1.6g - Protein: 29.5g

Ingredients:

- 2 (1-pound) salmon fillets
- Salt and freshly ground black pepper, to taste
- 1 tablespoon seafood seasoning
- 2 sliced lemons
- 2 sliced limes

Directions:

1. Preheat the pallet grill to 225 degrees F.
2. Season the salmon fillets with salt, black pepper and seafood seasoning evenly.
3. Place lemon and lime slices on top of each salmon fillet evenly.
4. Arrange the salmon fillets in pallet grill and cook for about 30 minutes.
5. Serve hot.

Strengthening Salmon (6 servings, serving: 1 portion)

Per Serving, Calories: 445- Fat: 29.2g - Carbs: 12.7g - Protein: 33.2g

Ingredients:

- 6 (6-ounce) skinless salmon fillets
- 1/3 cup olive oil
- ¼ cup spice rub
- ¼ cup honey
- 2 tablespoons Sriracha
- 2 tablespoons fresh lime juice

Directions:

1. Preheat the pallet grill to 300 degrees F.
2. Coat salmon fillets with olive oil and season with rub evenly.
3. In a small bowl, mix together remaining ingredients.
4. Arrange salmon fillets in pallet grill, flat-side up and cook for about 5-8 minute per side, coating with honey mixture once in the middle way.
5. Serve alongside remaining honey mixture.

Omega-3 Rich Salmon (4 servings, serving: 1 portion)

Per Serving, Calories: 181- Fat: 0.1g - Carbs: 28.5g - Protein: 8.2g

Ingredients:

- 2 cups soy sauce
- 1 cup dry white wine
- 1 cup water
- ½ teaspoon Tabasco sauce
- 1/3 cup sugar
- ¼ cup salt
- ½ teaspoon garlic powder
- ½ teaspoon onion powder
- Freshly ground black pepper, to taste
- 4 (6-ounce) salmon fillets

Directions:

For brine: in a large bowl, add all ingredients except salmon and stir till sugar is dissolved.

Add salmon fillets and refrigerate, covered overnight. Remove salmon from brine and rinse under cold water.

With paper towels, pat dry the trout fillets. Arrange a cooling rack in a sheet pan.

Place the salmon fillets onto cooling rack, skin side down and keep aside to cool for about 1 hour.

Preheat the pallet grill to 165 degrees F. Arrange the salmon fillets in pallet grill, skin side down and cook for about 3-5 hours or till desired doneness.

Time Saving Dinner (4 servings, serving: 1 portion)

Per Serving, Calories: 211- Fat: 8.6g - Carbs: 1g - Protein: 32.2g

Ingredients:

- 4 (6-ounce) mahi mahi fillets
- 2 tablespoons olive oil
- Salt and freshly ground black pepper, to taste

Directions:

1. Preheat the pallet grill to 350 degrees F.
2. Coat fish fillets with olive oil and season with salt and black pepper evenly.
3. Arrange fish fillets in pallet grill and cook for about 5 minutes per side.
4. Serve hot.

Nutritive Flounder (4 servings, serving: 1 portion)

Per Serving, Calories: 306- Fat: 16g - Carbs: 4.2g - Protein: 37.1g

Ingredients:

- ½ cup toasted sesame seeds
- ½ teaspoon kosher salt flakes
- 1 tablespoon canola oil
- 1 teaspoon sesame oil
- 4 (6-ounce) flounder fillets

Directions:

1. Preheat the pallet grill to 225 degrees F.
2. With a mortar and pestle, crush sesame seeds with kosher salt slightly.
3. In a small bowl, mix together both oils.
4. Coat fish fillets with oil mixture generously and then, rub with sesame seeds mixture.
5. Arrange fish fillets in the lower rack of pallet grill and cook, covered for about 2-2 ½ hours.
6. Serve hot.

Enjoyable Scallops (4 servings, serving: 1 portion)

Per Serving, Calories: 147- Fat: 5.5g - Carbs: 3.6g - Protein: 19.7g

Ingredients:

- 8 shelled and cleaned large scallops
- 8 extra thin prosciutto ham slices

Directions:

1. Preheat the pallet grill to 225-250 degrees F.
2. Arrange 1 scallop on the edge of a prosciutto slice and roll it up tucking in the sides of the prosciutto to cover completely.
3. Repeat with remaining scallops and prosciutto slices
4. Arrange the wrapped scallops onto a small wire rack.
5. Arrange wire rack in the pallet grill and cook for about 40 minutes.
6. Serve hot.

Appealing Shrimp (8 servings, serving: 1 portion)

Per Serving, Calories: 333- Fat: 16.8g - Carbs: 5.2g - Protein: 39.1g

Ingredients:

- 1 chopped onion
- 2 peeled garlic cloves
- 2 tablespoons peeled fresh ginger
- 2 tablespoons fresh cilantro
- ½ cup olive oil
- 2 teaspoons sesame oil
- ¼ cup fresh lemon juice
- Salt and freshly ground black pepper, to taste
- 3 pound peeled and deveined jumbo shrimp

Directions:

1. In a food processor, add all ingredients except shrimp and pulse till smooth.
2. Reserve ¼ of marinade in a small bowl.
3. Transfer remaining marinade into a baking dish with shrimp and toss to coat well.
4. Refrigerate, covered for about 1-2 hours. Preheat the pellet grill to 250 degrees F.
5. Remove shrimp from marinade and thread onto skewers.
6. Arrange the skewers in the pallet grill and cook for about 3-4 minutes per side, coating with reserved marinade occasionally.
7. Serve hot.

Lemony Shrimp (6 servings, serving: 1 portion)

Per Serving, Calories: 463- Fat: 33.3g - Carbs: 4.9g - Protein: 34.9g

Ingredients:

- 8-ounce melted salted butter
- ¼ cup Worcestershire sauce
- ¼ cup chopped fresh parsley
- 1 quartered lemon
- 2 pound peeled and deveined jumbo shrimp
- 3 tablespoons BBQ rub

Directions:

1. In a metal baking pan, add all ingredients except shrimp and rub and mix well.
2. Season shrimp with rub evenly.
3. Add shrimp in the pan with butter mixture and coat well.
4. Keep aside for about 20-30 minutes.
5. Preheat the pallet grill to 250 degrees F.
6. Arrange the pan in the pallet grill and cook for about 25-30 minutes.
7. Serve hot.

Yummy Prawns Treat (3 servings, serving: 1 portion)

Per Serving, Calories: 375- Fat: 15.6g - Carbs: 4.6g - Protein: 51.9g

Ingredients:

- ¼ cup finely minced fresh cilantro leaves
- 1 tablespoon crushed garlic
- 2½ tablespoons olive oil
- 2 tablespoons Thai chili sauce
- 1 tablespoon fresh lime juice
- 1½ pound peeled and deveined prawns

Directions:

1. In a large bowl, add all ingredients except prawns and mix well.
2. In a resealable plastic bag, add marinade and prawns.
3. Seal the bag and shake to coat well
4. Refrigerate, covered for about 20-30 minutes.
5. Preheat the pallet grill to 450 degrees F.
6. Remove prawns from marinade and thread onto skewers.
7. Arrange the skewers in the pallet grill and cook for about 4 minutes per side.
8. Serve hot.

Perfectly Grilled Lobster Tails (4 servings, serving: 1 portion)

Per Serving, Calories: 409- Fat: 24.9g - Carbs: 0.6g - Protein: 43.5g

Ingredients:

- ½ cup melted butter
- 2 minced garlic cloves
- 2 teaspoons fresh lemon juice
- Salt and freshly ground black pepper, to taste
- 4 (8-ounce) lobster tails

Directions:

1. Preheat the pallet grill to 450 degrees F.
2. In a metal pan, add all ingredients except lobster tails and mix well.
3. Arrange the pan in the pallet grill and cook for about 10 minutes.
4. Meanwhile, cut down the top of the shell and expose lobster meat.
5. Remove pan of butter mixture rom pallet grill.
6. Coat the lobster meat with butter mixture.
7. Arrange the lobster tails in pallet grill and cook for about 15 minutes, coating with butter mixture once in the middle way.
8. Serve hot.

Super-Tasty Clams (6 servings, serving: 1 portion)

Per Serving, Calories: 140- Fat: 15.4g - Carbs: 0.7g - Protein: 0.6g

Ingredients:

- 24 littleneck clams
- ½ cup chopped cold butter
- 2 tablespoons minced fresh parsley
- 3 finely minced garlic cloves
- 1 teaspoon fresh lemon juice

Directions:

1. Preheat the pallet grill to 450 degrees F.
2. Scrub the clams under cold running water.
3. In a large casserole dish, mix together remaining ingredients.
4. Place the pan in pallet grill.
5. Arrange the clams directly on the grill grate and cook for about 5-8 minutes or till they open.
6. Discard any that fail to open
7. With tongs, carefully transfer the opened clams into the casserole dish and remove from pallet grill.
8. Serve immediately.

Satisfying Meatballs (6 servings, serving: 1 portion)

Per Serving, Calories: 269- Fat: 8.3g - Carbs: 27.4g - Protein: 21.7g

Ingredients:

For Meatballs:

- 1¼ pound ground turkey
- 1 seeded and finely minced jalapeño pepper
- ½ cup panko breadcrumbs
- 1 beaten large egg
- ¼ cup milk
- ¼ teaspoon Worcestershire sauce
- 1 teaspoon onion powder
- 1 teaspoon garlic powder
- ¼ teaspoon chipotle rub
- ¼ teaspoon cayenne pepper
- Salt and freshly ground black pepper, to taste

For Glaze:

- 1 cup canned cranberry sauce
- ½ cup orange marmalade
- ½ cup chicken broth
- 1 tablespoon minced jalapeño pepper
- Salt and freshly ground black pepper, to taste

Directions:

1. For meatballs: in a large bowl, add all ingredients and mix till well combined.

2. With a plastic, cover the bowl and refrigerate for up to 1 hour.

3. Preheat the pallet grill to 350 degrees F.

4. With 1 tablespoon of turkey mixture, make balls.

5. Arrange the meatballs onto a parchment lined baking sheet in a single layer.

6. Arrange the pan in pallet grill and cook for about 10 minutes, flipping occasionally.

7. For glaze: in a small pan, add all ingredients and cook till well combined.

8. Remove from heat.

9. After 10 minutes, remove meatballs from pallet grill and coat with glaze evenly.

10. Half way through meatball cook time, brush the meatballs with the cranberry glaze.

11. Cook in the grill for about 10 minutes, flipping occasionally.

12. Serve hot.

Texas Style Sausage Poppers (4 servings, serving: 1 portion)

Per Serving, Calories: 576- Fat: 49.3g - Carbs: 2.3g - Protein: 29.7g

Ingredients:

- 1 pound sausage meat
- 5 jalapeño peppers
- ¾ cup grated cheddar cheese
- 4-ounce softened cream cheese

Directions:

1. Preheat the pallet grill to 250 degrees F.
2. Carefully, cut the top of each jalapeño pepper and remove the seeds and membrane.
3. In a bowl, add cheddar cheese and cream cheese and mix well.
4. Stuff each jalapeño pepper with cheese mixture.
5. Wrap some sausage meat around each jalapeño pepper to cover completely.
6. Arrange the poppers onto a pallet grill rack and cook for about 2 hours.
7. Serve hot.

Luncheon Turkey Burgers (4 servings, serving: 1 portion)

Per Serving, Calories: 344- Fat: 18.1g - Carbs: 2.4g - Protein: 40.7g

Ingredients:

- 1 pound ground chicken
- ½ cup chopped onion
- 2 tablespoons chopped fresh cilantro
- 1 minced chipotle chile in adobo sauce
- 1 tablespoon BBQ rub
- 1 teaspoon onion powder
- 1 teaspoon garlic powder
- 4 pepper jack cheese slices

Directions:

1. Preheat the pallet grill to 300 degrees F.
2. In a large bowl, add all ingredients except cheese and mix till well combined.
3. Make 4 equal sized 4 patties from mixture.
4. Arrange the patties in pallet grill and cook for about 7 minutes per side.
5. In the last minute of cooking, place1 cheese slice over each patty.

Flavorsome Cheeseburgers (4 servings, serving: 1 portion)

Per Serving, Calories: 213- Fat: 13.6g - Carbs: 0.7g - Protein: 20.6g

Ingredients:

- 2 pound ground chuck
- 1 cup grated Parmigiano-Reggiano
- Salt and freshly ground black pepper, to taste

Directions:

1. Preheat the pellet grill to 425 degrees F.
2. In a bowl, add all ingredients and mix well.
3. Make 4 (¾-inch thick) patties from mixture.
4. With your thumbs, make a shallow but wide depression in each patty.
5. Arrange the patties in pallet grill grate, depression-side down and cook for about 8 minutes.
6. Flip and cook for about 8-10 minutes.
7. Serve immediately.

Earthy Flavored Meatloaf (20 servings, serving: 1 portion)

Per Serving, Calories: 456- Fat: 23.4g - Carbs: 10.7g - Protein: 48.1g

Ingredients:

For Meatloaf:

- 5 pound ground beef
- 2 pound broken into chunks sausage
- 4 eggs
- 1 chopped onion
- 1 cup breadcrumbs
- 1 (8-ounce) jar chunky salsa
- ¼ cup shredded parmesan cheese
- ¼ cup BBQ sauce
- ¼ cup ketchup
- ¼ cup mustard
- 2 tablespoons malt vinegar
- 2 tablespoons soy sauce
- 2 tablespoons Sriracha sauce
- 1 (1¼-ounce) package meatloaf seasoning mix
- 1 tablespoon garlic powder
- Salt and freshly ground black pepper, to taste

For Topping:

- 2 tablespoons BBQ sauce
- 2 tablespoons BBQ glaze
- 2 tablespoons ketchup
- 2 tablespoons mustard
- 1 teaspoon Worcestershire sauce

Directions:

1. For meatloaf in a large bowl, add all ingredients and mix till well combined.
2. Place the meat mixture into a plastic wrap lined container and press to form a meatloaf.
3. Refrigerate for about 3-4 hours or till set.
4. Preheat the pallet grill to 250 degrees F, using charcoal.
5. Line a wire rack with a piece of foil and arrange in a foil lined baking pan.
6. With the plastic wrap, carefully lift the meatloaf and arrange into prepared rack.
7. Place the baking pan in pallet grill and cook for about 3 hours.
8. Meanwhile in in a bowl, mix together all topping ingredients.
9. Coat the meatloaf with topping mixture.
10. Cook for about 1-2 hours more.
11. Remove meatloaf from pallet grill and keep aside for about 10 minutes before serving.
12. Cut into desired sized slices and serve.

Great Meat Combo Loaf (10 servings, serving: 1 portion)

Per Serving, Calories: 433- Fat: 20.8g - Carbs: 22.1g - Protein: 39.5g

Ingredients:

- 1½ cups BBQ sauce, divided
- 1¼ pound ground turkey
- 1¼ pound ground beef chuck
- 1 pound ground pork
- 2 chopped roasted bell peppers
- 1/3 cup finely chopped onion
- 4 minced garlic cloves
- 2 beaten eggs
- ¾ cup fresh breadcrumbs
- 1 tablespoon crushed dried oregano
- Salt and freshly ground black pepper, to taste

Directions:

Preheat the pallet grill to 225 degrees F.

In a large bowl, add ½ cup of BBQ sauce and remaining all ingredients and mix till well combined.

Arrange a 24-inch piece of foil in a small baking sheet, doubling it over by folding it half and then, mold the sides of foil upwards to make a loaf pan.

Place the meat mixture in loaf pan and press to form a meatloaf. Place the loaf pan over pallet grill rack and cook for about 3-4 hours.

In the last hour of coking, coat the meatloaf with the remaining BBQ sauce. Remove meatloaf from pallet grill and keep aside for about 10 minutes before serving. Cut into desired sized slices and serve.

Nicely Charred Meatloaf (8 servings, serving: 1 portion)

Per Serving, Calories: 432- Fat: 12.9g - Carbs: 21.3g - Protein: 55.9g

Ingredients:

For Meatloaf:

- 3 pound ground beef
- 3 eggs
- ½ cup panko breadcrumbs
- 1 (10 ounce) can diced tomatoes with green chile peppers
- 1 chopped large white onion
- 2 chopped hot banana peppers
- 2 tablespoons seasoned salt
- 2 teaspoons liquid smoke flavoring
- 2 teaspoons smoked paprika
- 1 teaspoons onion salt
- 1 teaspoons garlic salt
- Salt and freshly ground black pepper, to taste

For Sauce:

- ½ cup ketchup
- ¼ cup tomato-based chile sauce
- ¼ cup white sugar
- 2 teaspoons Worcestershire sauce

- 2 teaspoons hot pepper sauce
- 1 teaspoon red pepper flakes
- 1 teaspoon red chili pepper
- Salt and freshly ground black pepper, to taste

Directions:

1. Preheat the pallet grill to 225 degrees F.
2. Grease a loaf pan.
3. For meatloaf: in a bowl, add all ingredients and with your hands, mix till well combined.
4. Place the mixture into prepared loaf pan evenly.
5. Arrange the pan in pallet grill and cook for about 2 hours.
6. For sauce: in a bowl, add all ingredients and beat till well combined.
7. Remove pan from pallet grill and drain excess grease from meatloaf.
8. Place sauce over meatloaf evenly and cook in pallet grill for about 30 minutes.
9. Remove meatloaf from pallet grill and keep aside for about 10 minutes before serving.
10. Cut into desired sized slices and serve.

Award Winning Pot Pie (10 servings, serving: 1 portion)

Per Serving, Calories: 318- Fat: 17.8g - Carbs: 13.4g - Protein: 29.7g

Ingredients:

- 2 tablespoons cornstarch
- 2 tablespoons water
- 3 cups chicken broth
- 1 cup milk
- 3 tablespoons butter
- 1 tablespoon chopped fresh rosemary
- 1 tablespoon chopped fresh thyme
- Salt and freshly ground black pepper, to taste
- 4 cups cooked ground turkey
- 2 cups frozen chopped broccoli
- 1½ cups frozen peas
- 1½ cups frozen chopped carrots
- 1 frozen puff pastry sheet

Directions:

Preheat the pallet grill to 375 degrees F. In a small bowl dissolve cornstarch in water. Keep aside. In a pan, add broth, milk, butter and herbs and bring to a boil.

add cornstarch mixture and stir to combine well. Stir in salt and black pepper and remove from heat. In a large bowl, add turkey, frozen vegetables and sauce and mix well.

Transfer mixture into a cast iron skillet. Cover the mixture with the puff pastry and cut excess from edges. Arrange the skillet in pallet grill and cook for about 1 hour and 20 minutes.

Remove from pallet grill and keep aside for about 15 minutes before serving. Cut into desired sized portions and serve.

Mexican Stuffed Peppers (6 servings, serving: 1

Per Serving, Calories: 563- Fat: 6.6g - Carbs: 88.8g - Protein: 37.2g

Ingredients:

- 6 large red bell peppers
- 1 pound ground beef
- 1 chopped small onion
- 2 minced garlic cloves
- 2 cups cooked rice
- 1 cup corn
- 1 cup cooked black beans
- 2/3 cup salsa
- 2 tablespoons Cajun rub
- 1½ cups grated Monterey Jack cheese

Directions:

Preheat the pallet grill to 350 degrees F. Cut each bell pepper in half lengthwise through the stem.

Carefully, remove the seeds and ribs. For stuffing: heat a large frying pan and cook the beef till browned completely.

Add onion and garlic and sauté for about 2-3 minutes. Stir in remaining ingredients except cheese and cook for about 5 minutes. Stuff each bell pepper half with stuffing mixture evenly.

Arrange the peppers in pallet grill, stuffing side up and for about 40 minutes. Sprinkle each pepper half with cheese and cook for about 5 minutes.

Serve immediately.

Fancy Party Time Treat (6 servings, serving: 1 portion)

Per Serving, Calories: 268- Fat: 14g - Carbs: 18.1g - Protein: 17.8g

Ingredients:

- 1 pound stems removed large mushrooms
- ½ pound ground Italian sausage
- 4-ounce seasoned bread crumbs
- 4-ounce shredded parmesan cheese
- 1 cup chopped fresh spinach
- 2 tablespoons finely chopped onion
- 1 teaspoon minced garlic

Directions:

1. Preheat the pallet grill to 400 degrees F.
2. Arrange mushrooms caps in nonstick pan.
3. In a large bowl, add remaining ingredients and mix well.
4. Stuff each mushroom cap with cheese mixture.
5. Arrange the pan in pallet grill and cook for about 30 minutes.
6. Serve hot.

Comforting Casserole (8 servings, serving: 1 portion)

Per Serving, Calories: 472- Fat: 27.8g - Carbs: 21.7g - Protein: 32.5g

Ingredients:

- 2 (15-ounce) cans cream of chicken soup
- 2 cups milk
- 2 tablespoons unsalted butter
- ¼ cup all-purpose flour
- 1 pound chopped skinless, boneless chicken thighs
- ½ cup chopped hatch chiles
- 2 chopped medium onions
- 1 tablespoon chopped fresh thyme
- Salt and freshly ground black pepper, to taste
- 1 cup chopped cooked bacon
- 1 cup tater tots

Directions:

Preheat the pallet grill to 400 degrees F. In a large bowl, mix together chicken soup and milk. In a skillet, melt butter on medium heat.

Slowly, add flour, stirring continuously till smooth. Slowly, add soup mixture, beating continuously till smooth. Cook till mixture starts to thicken, stirring continuously.

Stir in remaining ingredients except bacon and simmer for about 10-15 minutes. Stir in bacon and transfer mixture into a 2½-quart casserole dish. Place tater tots on top of casserole evenly.

Arrange the pan in pallet grill and cook for about 30-35 minutes. Serve hot.

Creamy Casserole (10 servings, serving: 1 portion)

Per Serving, Calories: 154- Fat: 10.7g - Carbs: 14.6g - Protein: 2.3g

Ingredients:

- 5 tablespoons olive oil, divided
- 6 cups thinly sliced onions
- 1 tablespoon chopped fresh thyme, divided
- Salt and freshly ground black pepper, to taste
- 1 tablespoon unsalted butter
- 1¼ pound peeled and 1/8-inch thick sliced Yukon gold potatoes
- ½ cup heavy cream
- 2¼ pound ¼-inch thick sliced tomatoes

Directions:

1. In a large cast iron pan, heat 3 tablespoons of oil and on high heat and cook onions, 1 teaspoon of thyme, salt and black pepper for about 5 minutes stirring occasionally.
2. Reduce the heat to medium.
3. Add butter and cook for about 15 minutes.
4. Reduce the heat to low and cook for about 10 minutes.
5. Preheat the pallet grill to 350 degrees F.
6. Meanwhile in a bowl, add potatoes slices, cream, 1 teaspoon of thyme, salt and black pepper and toss to coat.
7. In another bowl, add tomato slices, salt and black pepper and toss to coat.

8. Transfer half of the caramelized onions into a small bowl.

9. spread the remaining half in the bottom of the cast iron pan evenly and top with 1 layer of potatoes and tomatoes.

10. Drizzle with 2 tablespoons of cream from potatoes and 1 tablespoon of olive oil.

11. Sprinkle with a little salt, black pepper and ½ teaspoon of thyme.

12. Spread remaining caramelized onions on top, followed by potatoes and tomatoes.

13. Drizzle with remaining cream from the potatoes and remaining tablespoon olive oil.

14. Sprinkle with a little salt, black pepper and remaining ½ teaspoon of thyme.

15. With a piece of foil, cover the cast iron pan tightly.

16. Arrange the pan in pallet grill and cook for about 2 hours.

17. Remove from the pallet grill and uncover the cast iron pan.

18. Now, set the pallet grill to 450 degrees F.

19. Arrange the cast iron, uncovered in pallet grill and cook for about 25-30 minutes.

20. Serve hot.

Classic Mac & Cheese (12 servings, serving: 1 portion)

Per Serving, Calories: 72- Fat: 35.2g - Carbs: 83.3g - Protein: 31g

Ingredients:

- 2 pound elbow macaroni
- ¾ cup butter
- ½ cup flour
- 1 teaspoon dry mustard
- 1½ cups milk
- 2 pound cut into ½-inch cubes Velveeta cheese
- Salt and freshly ground black pepper, to taste
- 1½ cups shredded cheddar cheese
- 2 cups plain dry breadcrumbs
- Paprika, to taste

Directions:

1. Preheat the pallet grill to 350 degrees F.
2. In a large pan of lightly salted boiling water, cook macaroni for about 7-8 minutes.
3. Drain well, and transfer into a large bowl.
4. Meanwhile, in a medium pan, melt 8 tablespoons of butter on medium heat.
5. Slowly, add flour and mustard, beating continuously till smooth.
6. Cook for about 2 minutes, beating continuously.
7. Slowly, add milk, beating continuously till smooth.
8. Reduce the heat to medium-low and slowly, stir in Velveeta cheese till melted.
9. Stir in salt and black pepper and remove from heat.
10. Place cheese sauce over cooked macaroni and gently, stir to combine.
11. Place the macaroni mixture into greased casserole dish evenly and sprinkle with cheddar cheese.
12. In a small frying pan, melt remaining 4 tablespoons of butter.
13. Stir in breadcrumbs and remove from heat.
14. Place breadcrumbs mixture over cheddar cheese evenly and sprinkle with paprika lightly.
15. Arrange the casserole dish in pallet grill and cook for about 45-60 minutes, turning the pan once in the middle way.
16. Serve hot.

Cheesy Corn (12 servings, serving: 1 portion)

Per Serving, Calories: 873- Fat: 33g - Carbs: 128.1g - Protein: 38g

Ingredients:

- 6 bacon strips
- ½ of seeded and chopped green bell pepper
- ½ of seeded and chopped red bell pepper
- ½ of chopped onion
- 52-ounce frozen corn
- 3-4 cup shredded cheddar cheese
- 8-ounce cream cheese
- Salt and freshly ground black pepper, to taste

Directions:

1. Preheat the pallet grill to 275-350 degrees F.
2. Heat a skillet on medium-high heat and cook bacon for about 8-10 minutes.
3. Transfer the bacon onto a paper towel lined plate to drain, leaving grease in skillet.
4. Chop the bacon and keep aside.
5. In the same skillet, add bel peppers and onion and sauté for about 4-5 minutes.
6. Remove from heat and stir in remaining ingredients.
7. Transfer the mixture in to an aluminum pan evenly.
8. Arrange the pan I pallet grill and cook for about 1-2 hours, stirring after every 30 minutes.

Old-Fashioned Beans (16 servings, serving: 1 portion)

Per Serving, Calories: 478- Fat: 7.4g - Carbs: 77.3g - Protein: 27.7g

Ingredients:

- 8 chopped bacon strips
- ½ of seeded and chopped red bell pepper
- ½ of chopped medium onion
- 2 chopped jalapeño peppers
- 1 (55-ounce) can baked beans
- 8-ounce drained pineapple chunks
- 1 cup BBQ sauce
- 1 cup brown sugar
- 1 tablespoon ground mustard

Directions:

1. Preheat the pallet grill to 220-250 degrees F.
2. Heat a skillet on medium-high heat and cook bacon for about 8-10 minutes.
3. Transfer the bacon onto a paper towel lined plate to drain, leaving grease in skillet.
4. In the same skillet, add bel peppers, onion and jalapeño peppers and sauté for about 4-5 minutes.
5. Remove from heat and transfer into a bowl. Add remaining ingredients and stir to combine. Transfer the mixture into a Dutch oven.
6. Arrange the Dutch oven in pallet grill and cook for about 2½-3 hours.
7. Serve hot.

Super-Fun Potatoes (6 servings, serving: 1 portion)

Per Serving, Calories: 625- Fat: 42.3g - Carbs: 40.7g - Protein: 22.1g

Ingredients:

- 6 russet potatoes
- 2 tablespoons olive oil
- Salt, to taste
- 8 cooked and crumbled bacon slices
- ½ cup heavy whipping cream
- 4-ounce softened cream cheese
- 4 tablespoons softened butter
- 4 seeded and chopped jalapeño peppers
- 1 teaspoon seasoned salt
- 2 cups grated Monterrey Jack cheese, divided

Directions:

Preheat the pallet grill to 225 degrees F. With paper towels, pat dry the washed potatoes completely. Coat the potatoes with olive oil sprinkle with some salt.

Arrange potatoes in pellet grill and cook for about 3-3½ hours. Remove the potatoes from pellet grill and cut them in half lengthwise.

With a large spoon carefully, scoop out the potato flesh from skins, leaving a little potato layer. In a large bowl, add potato flesh and mash it slightly.

Add bacon, cream, cream cheese, butter, jalapeno, seasoned salt and 1 cup of Monterrey Jack cheese and gently, stir to combine. stuff the potato skins with bacon mixture and top with remaining Monterrey Jack cheese.

Arrange the stuffed potatoes onto a baking sheet. Arrange the baking sheet in pellet grill and cook for about 30 minutes.

Serve hot.

Irish Bread (10 servings, serving: 1 portion)

Per Serving, Calories: 340- Fat: 6.6g - Carbs: 63g - Protein: 8.6g

Ingredients:

- 4 cups flour
- 1 cup raisins
- ½ cup sugar
- 1 tablespoon caraway seeds
- 2 teaspoons baking powder
- 1 teaspoon baking soda
- ¾ teaspoon salt
- 1¼ cups buttermilk
- 1 cup sour cream
- 2 eggs

Directions:

1. Preheat the pallet grill to 350 degrees F.
2. Grease a 9-inch round cake pan.
3. Reserve 1 tablespoon of flour in a bowl.
4. In a large bowl, mix together remaining flour, raisins, sugar, caraway seeds, baking powder, baking soda and salt.
5. In another small bowl, add buttermilk, sour cream and eggs and beat till well combined.
6. Add egg mixture into flour mixture and mix till just moistened.

7. With your hands, knead the dough till sticky.

8. Place the dough in the prepared pan evenly and cut a 4x¾-inch deep slit in the top.

9. Dust the top with reserved flour.

10. Arrange the pan in pallet grill and cook for about 1½ hours or till a toothpick inserted in the center comes out clean.

11. Remove from pallet grill and keep onto a wire rack to cool in the pan for about 10 minutes.

12. Carefully, invert the bread onto wire rack to cool completely before slicing.

13. Cut the bread into desired slices and sere.

Southern Cornbread (8 servings, serving: 1 portion)

Per Serving, Calories: 527- Fat: 11.8g - Carbs: 90g - Protein: 14.9g

Ingredients:

- 2 tablespoons melted butter
- 1½ cups all-purpose flour
- 1½ cups ground yellow cornmeal
- 2 tablespoons sugar
- 3 teaspoons baking powder
- ¾ teaspoon baking soda
- ¾ teaspoon salt
- 1 cup whole milk
- 1 cup buttermilk
- 3 large eggs
- 3 tablespoons melted butter

Directions:

1. Preheat the pallet grill to 400 degrees F.
2. In a 13x9-inch baking dish, place 2 tablespoon of butter.
3. Place the baking dish in pellet grill to melt butter and heat up pan.
4. In a large bowl, mix together flour, cornmeal, sugar, baking powder, baking soda and salt.

5. In another bowl, add milk, buttermilk, eggs and melted butter and beat till well combined.

6. Add egg mixture into flour mixture and mix till just moistened.

7. Place the mixture into heated baking dish evenly.

8. Arrange the pan in pallet grill and cook for about 20 minutes or till a toothpick inserted in the center comes out clean.

9. Remove from pallet grill and keep onto a wire rack to cool in the pan for about 10 minutes.

10. Carefully, invert the bread onto wire rack to cool completely before slicing.

11. Cut the bread into desired slices and sere.

Fall Time Apple Pie (8 servings, serving: 1 portion)

Per Serving, Calories: 252- Fat: 7.2g - Carbs: 48.8g - Protein: 1.3g

Ingredients:

For Filling:

- 1 (9-inch) frozen double crust
- ¾ cup sugar
- 1 tablespoon all-purpose flour
- 1 teaspoon ground cinnamon
- Pinch of salt
- 3½ cups, peeled, cored and chopped cooking apples
- 16-ounce applesauce
- 1 tablespoon fresh lemon juice
- 2 tablespoons chopped cold butter

For Topping:

- 3 tablespoons all-purpose flour
- 1 tablespoon sugar
- Pinch of salt
- 1 tablespoon butter

Directions:

1. Preheat the pellet grill to 400 degrees F.
2. Place half of dough in the bottom of a 9-inch pie plate.
3. For topping: in a bowl, mix together sugar, flour, cinnamon and salt.
4. Add apples, applesauce and lemon juice and stir to combine.
5. Place apple mixture into pie pan and top with butter in the shape of dots.
6. Cut remaining crust into strips and place over pie in a lattice pattern.
7. For topping: in a bowl, mix together flour, sugar and salt.
8. With a fork, cut in butter till a crumbly mixture is formed
9. Sprinkle topping mixture over top of crust evenly.
10. Arrange the pie plate in pallet grill and cook for about 10 minutes.
11. Now, set the pallet grill to 350 degrees F and cook for about 45 minutes.
12. Remove from the oven and keep onto a wire rack to cool in the pan for about 10 minutes.
13. Serve warm.

Sweet Tooth Carving Crunch (8 servings, serving: 1 portion)

Per Serving, Calories: 382- Fat: 12.5g - Carbs: 66.3g - Protein: 3.7g

Ingredients:

- 1 cup oatmeal
- 1 cup flour
- I cup brown sugar
- ½ cup melted butter
- ½ teaspoon salt
- 4 cups finely chopped raw rhubarb
- 1 cup white sugar
- 2 tablespoons cornstarch
- 1 cup cold water
- 1 teaspoon vanilla extract

Directions:

1. Preheat the pallet grill to 350 degrees F.
2. In a bowl, add oatmeal, flour, brown sugar, butter and salt and mix till well combined.
3. In a pan, add white sugar, cornstarch, cold water and vanilla extract and cook till sugar is dissolves, stirring continuously. Place half of four mixture into a 9x12-inch pan and top with chopped rhubarb evenly.
4. Place sugar mixture over rhubarb evenly and top with remaining flour mixture.
5. Arrange the pan in pallet grill and cook for about 1 hour.
6. Serve warm.

Chocolate Lover's Cheesecake (8 servings, serving: 1 portion)

Per Serving, Calories: 605- Fat: 3.94g - Carbs: 68.3g - Protein: 8.3g

Ingredients:

For Base:

- 1 cup chocolate wafer crumbs
- 2 tablespoons melted butter

For Filling:

- 4-ounce unsweetened baking chocolate
- 16-ounce softened cream cheese
- ¾ cup white sugar
- 2 eggs
- 1 teaspoon vanilla extract

For Topping:

- ¼ cup heavy cream
- 2-ounce finely chopped unsweetened baking chocolate
- ¼ cup white sugar
- 1 tablespoon unsalted butter

Directions:

1. Preheat the pallet grill to 325 degrees F.
2. For base: in a bowl, mix together wafer crumbs and melted butter.
3. Line an 8-inch spring form pan with parchment paper.
4. Place the crumb mixture in the bottom of prepared spring form pan and press to fit.
5. Arrange the pan in pallet grill and cook for about 10 minutes.
6. Remove pan from pallet grill and keep aside to cool.
7. For filling: in a microwave-safe bowl, add chocolate and microwave till melted.
8. Remove from microwave and keep aside to cool slightly.
9. In another bowl, add cream cheese and sugar and beat till light and fluffy.
10. Add eggs, one at a time, beating after each addition.
11. Add melted chocolate and vanilla extract and mix well.
12. Place filling mixture over cooled base evenly and cook in pallet grill for about 45-50 minutes.
13. Remove from pallet grill and keep onto a wire rack to cool.
14. For topping: in a heavy bottomed pan, heat heavy cream on medium heat.
15. Add chocolate, sugar and butter and cook till sugar dissolves, stirring continuously.
16. Remove from heat and keep aside to cool slightly.
17. Pour chocolate mixture over the cooled cheesecake evenly.
18. Refrigerate for at least 4 hours before serving

Kid's Favorite Brownies (20 servings, serving: 1 portion)

Per Serving, Calories: 182- Fat: 7.2g - Carbs: 28.2g - Protein: 2.2g

Ingredients:

- 4-ounce unsweetened chocolate squares
- ½ cup butter
- 2 cups white sugar
- 4 eggs
- 1 teaspoon pure vanilla extract
- ¼ teaspoon salt
- 1 cup unbleached white flour

Directions:

Preheat the pallet grill to 350 degrees F.

Grease a 9x13-invch baking pan.

In a microwave-safe bowl, add chocolate and butter and microwave till melted. Remove from microwave and keep aside to cool.

In another bowl, add eggs, sugar vanilla and salt and with a hand mixer, beat till light and fluffy.

Add cooled chocolate mixture and stir till well combined. Add flour and mix till just combined.

Place the mixture into prepared pan and with the back of a spoon, smooth the surface.

Arrange the pan on the lower rack of pallet grill and cook, covered for about 25 minutes. Remove from pallet grill and keep onto a wire rack to cool completely.

Cut into desired sized squared and serve.

Final Words

Thank you again for picking up this cookbook! I hope it was able to help you to find a wide variety of simple, and delicious sounding recipes that you can't wait to try for yourself.

Finally, if you enjoyed this book, then I'd like to ask you for a favor, would you be kind enough to leave a review for this book on Amazon? It'd be greatly appreciated!

Made in the USA
Middletown, DE
12 May 2020